EVANGELICALS ARE POWERLESS

The Truth About Salvation & Spirit
Baptism You Won't Learn in Church

BY

JOHN D. HUGHES

~ Spotless Books ~

EVANGELICALS ARE POWERLESS
Copyright © 2025 John D. Hughes

Published by Spotless Books, Houston, TX

All rights reserved. No part of this publication may be copied or reproduced in any form, stored in or introduced into any storage or retrieval system, or shared in any form or by any means—except for brief quotations in critical reviews or articles—without the prior written permission of the author.

Evangelicals Are Powerless: The Truth About Salvation & Spirit Baptism You Won't Learn in Church

Unless otherwise noted, scripture quotations are taken from the (NASB®) New American Standard Bible®, Copyright © 2020 by The Lockman Foundation. Used by permission. All rights reserved. lockman.org. Scripture quotations marked (NLT) are taken from the Holy Bible, New Living Translation, copyright ©1996, 2004, 2015 by Tyndale House Foundation. Used by permission of Tyndale House Publishers, Carol Stream, Illinois 60188. All rights reserved. In some cases, the author has added bold-face type to scripture quotations for emphasis, as well as bracketed insertions for explanatory information.

All references to the definitions/meanings of specific biblical Hebrew or biblical Greek words come from either Strong's Exhaustive Concordance to the Bible or the Bible Hub website (www.biblehub.com).

Connect with the author: Facebook: facebook.com/groups/hugheswriter/

Cover design by www.markkaris.com

ISBN: 978-1-7322426-4-7
978-1-7322426-5-4 (eBooks)

Library of Congress Control Number: 2025903426

Printed in the United States of America

First Edition

10 9 8 7 6 5 4 3 2 1

It was for freedom that Christ set us free;
therefore keep standing firm and do not
be subject again to a yoke of slavery.

GALATIANS 5:1

Do not quench the Spirit, do not utterly
reject prophecies, but examine everything;
hold firmly to that which is good.

1 THESSALONIANS 5:19-21

Table of Contents

Preface 1
Introduction. 15

FOUNDATION CHAPTERS | 19

1: The Truth About Salvation 21
2: The Truth About Water Baptism 37
3: Get to Know the Holy Spirit 57
4: The Truth About the Book of Acts 93

CORE CHAPTERS | 147

5: The Three Baptisms of Jesus 149
6: The Three Baptisms of the Disciples. 177
7: The Three Baptisms of Believers Today. 217

APPLICATION CHAPTERS | 249

8: How to Be Truly Saved. 251
9: How to Be Baptized in Water. 259
10: How to Be Baptized in the Holy Spirit. 265
A Final Word: From My Heart to Yours 273

Preface

Don't Believe Everything Your Pastor Says
This book will change your faith and your life. No, not the book you're holding. The Bible, the very Word of God. The book you're holding will help make that happen.

Evangelicals Are Powerless will reveal biblical truths that you likely have never been taught, especially truths about salvation, baptisms, spiritual power, and freedom in Christ.

I know this is possible because what I share in this book changed my life. The key is to only believe the Word of God, nothing else and no one else.

Let me be clear: Go to church! Listen to your pastor. But don't just believe everything they say. And don't believe everything your Sunday school teacher says. Or your Bible study leader. Or a TV preacher. Or a friend. Or an author. Including me. Take what you hear and search the scriptures for yourself. Trust God and His Word alone.

Here's my story…

❦

Thirty-six years.
From 1981 to 2017.
That's 1,872 Sundays.

Sunday after Sunday. Week after week. Year after year.

That's how long I sat in the pews of nondenominational, evangelical churches listening to hundreds and hundreds of sermons, believing I was being taught the entirety of the Bible—the truth, the whole truth, and nothing but the truth.

But I wasn't.

Not even close.

On Sunday afternoon, May 14, 2017, at fifty-four years old, I finally began to understand that I had been misled. Cheated, even. I had missed out on learning and understanding most of scripture. And worse, I missed out on a deeper faith and relationship with God and His Son, as well as understanding pretty much anything about the Holy Spirit, including the power that He had waiting for me throughout those thirty-six years.

Please hear me: No pastor deliberately misled or cheated me. I know that. They simply taught and preached what they had learned, and they did it with a heart for Jesus. I would not have been saved if that wasn't the case.

However, I'd been kept on baby's milk and never fed the meat of scripture—meat that builds understanding, discernment, and faith:

> For everyone who partakes only of milk is unacquainted with the word of righteousness, for he is an infant. (Hebrews 5:13)

> So faith comes from hearing, and hearing by the word of Christ. (Romans 10:17)

It was as if those evangelical pastors and teachers were saying, "You're saved and baptized in water. That's all you need. That's all that matters. There isn't anything more for you to know or understand or receive."

They were so very wrong. There is, in fact, much more to know and understand and receive. I have personally experienced this "more" over the last eight years, and I want you to experience it as well.

In this book, I will share with you the scriptural details of what I learned and received that so profoundly changed my faith and life.

Over those thirty-six years, I had swallowed all that was fed to me from the pulpit hook, line, and sinker—regardless of what church I was in or who was preaching. I fully trusted that those preachers and teachers weren't leaving anything out—at least, nothing important.

The overwhelming majority of believers sitting in churches today are taking the same bait: They are being cheated in sermon after sermon, Sunday after Sunday, year after year. They are missing out on greater faith and spiritual power:

> And He gave some as apostles, some as prophets, some as evangelists, some as pastors and teachers, for the equipping of the saints for the work of ministry, for the building up of the body of Christ. (Ephesians 4:11-12)

In terms of teaching the Word of God, most pastors today focus more on lifestyle teaching than teaching deep biblical truths. Very few teach a full and accurate scripture, instead teaching an inaccurate Word of God and an incorrect gospel.

I realize you may not believe me, but read this book, discover what the Bible actually says, and then decide for yourself whether to believe your pastor or the Bible.

Once you see it—the truth of God's Word—your faith and life will change. How you read the Bible will change. How you understand the Bible will change. How you see Jesus will change. I warn you, though, once you do see it, you will feel betrayed at first, as if all those pastors and preachers and Bible teachers misled you—and how your life could have been so different if you'd had this understanding from the start. But once you see it, you can't unsee it. You will crave more of the truth of God's Word, more of God Himself, more of Jesus and what He *actually* did for you, and more of the Holy Spirit—the God you likely do not know.

This isn't just speculation on my part. I have watched well over a hundred sermons online in just the past year—dozens of different preachers and teachers from dozens of different denominations and churches. I have also listened to over fifty sermons in person by at least twenty different preachers over that same time frame. Only a couple of them had a good understanding of scripture. Here are just four examples of what I heard in Christian churches over the past 12 months:

First, during one sermon, a pastor showed the congregation a slide with these exact words on it:

> Jesus will return and
> He will judge the world.
> Jesus was convinced of it.

Huh? I'm convinced that Jesus didn't need convincing—*of anything*. He not only wrote scripture, but He was, is, and always will be the very *Word of God*! And this certainly includes knowing that He Himself would in fact return and judge the world (via two separate judgments to be clear). And He knew this before time began.

Next, a pastor at a different church told the congregation that after Jesus ascended, the disciples went out and fulfilled the Great Commission, as recorded in the book of Acts.

But they didn't. Not even close. Instead, Acts recounts that they remained in Jerusalem:

> Now Saul approved of putting Stephen to death. And on that day a great persecution began against the church in Jerusalem, and they were all scattered throughout the regions of Judea and Samaria, **except for the apostles**. (Acts 8:1)

Stephen was stoned about a year after Christ's death. Even then the Jewish followers of Jesus went only as far as Samaria, a little north of Jerusalem. And none of the original disciples ventured out of the city. Most never made it any farther into the world until God forced them out in AD 70—nearly *forty years* after Jesus gave them the Great Commission. And, except for Peter going to Cornelius's house (Acts 10), *none* of the disciples went to the Gentiles—they preached only to Jews.

At still another church, I learned that the pastor had been preaching from the book of Mark for two years. Now, there is nothing wrong with the book of Mark. It's the Word of God, after all! But the four gospels were written to Jews, not Gentiles. Christians today cannot be equipped through the gospels. As we'll see in later chapters, Jesus Himself made it clear that His earthly ministry was for the Israelite nation only.

And one final example: Another pastor said, "Jesus didn't just die on the cross for you two thousand years ago; he's actually still continuously pouring out His blood on your behalf."

No. He isn't.

Christ died, was buried, and rose again. He *fully* finished His work on the cross. His blood stopped flowing two thousand years ago. To say His blood continues to flow keeps Jesus nailed to the cross. He's no longer there because He rose three days later, defeating sin and death for all time.

Preachers and teachers need to preach and teach the real Jesus. And instead of spending two years in the gospels, preach and teach also from Paul's letters, which contain the teachings and doctrines that Christians are to follow today. We are not called to follow Jesus's earthly ministry. In fact, as you will learn, it's actually impossible to do that. We are certainly called to *behave* like Jesus, which should happen naturally through the fruit of the Spirit in us. (Galatians 5:22-23) Instead, in this current age of God's grace, we are to follow the teachings of the apostle Paul, which he received *directly from Jesus*. If we learn from and follow Paul's teachings, we follow Jesus:

> And you should imitate me, just as I imitate Christ. (1 Corinthians 11:1 NLT)

I know this may sound like heresy, but I promise you, it's not. It is biblical truth. Read on to learn what most pastors and Bible teachers don't understand about scripture.

What these four pastors taught wasn't heretical, but it showed a lack of understanding God's Word and, worse, a lack of knowing who Jesus was and is. To be clear, this book is *not* about exposing pastors but about exposing the truth of the Word of God, the faith it builds, and the power it holds for believers of Jesus Christ.

But, please, don't take my word for it. I encourage you to read this book and use it as a guide to search the scriptures and decide for yourself what God said and who Jesus was and is.

Once I understood the truth of scripture, which I share in this book, the Bible finally made sense. I certainly don't understand everything, but I know who Jesus truly is now. I know why He said the strange and confusing things He did, like calling a woman a "dog" in Matthew 15:26. Why the apostle Paul, in Romans 16, called the gospel he preached, "My gospel." Why there seem to be so many different types of salvations and baptisms in the New Testament, many of which contradict each other. And why Acts 2 is so pivotal for believers today yet so controversial at the same time.

We'll cover each of these topics in this book to bring greater clarity to God's Word, which will in turn grow your understanding and faith. I will also show you the truth about salvation and the unequivocal biblical basis for the baptism in the Holy Spirit that most Christians are missing today.

God not only sent His Son to give us eternal salvation and the Holy Spirit to live *in* us, but He also promised to give us a separate and distinct *outpouring* of the Holy Spirit. It's this outpouring that brings power for witnessing and supernatural power for prophesying and building up the Body of Christ. Scripture is clear on this; I will show you.

God intended for you and me to have this power for today just as much as He intended it for first-century believers. He did not intend for us to labor alone in faith under our own meager human efforts. Our weakness only brings struggle and failure.

On that Sunday afternoon in May of 2017, I watched a sermon on Christian TV. The pastor was doing a deep dive into the person and work of the Holy Spirit. In that sermon, he gave me a tiny glimpse of what I'd been missing both scripturally and from a faith perspective. And a tiny glimpse was all I needed. I took it and ran with it. I dove deep into my Bible looking for more of the gold nuggets of God's truth that I'd been missing. I started watching multiple sermons every week and reading through books and articles. My understanding of scripture grew faster and deeper in those few weeks and months than it had throughout the previous thirty-six years. And so did my faith and understanding of God, Jesus, and the Holy Spirit.

I remember the exact moment everything changed for me. That TV preacher leaned toward his congregation and said something like, "I don't see any way you can get around that verse. You may not agree with speaking in tongues [which I didn't at the time], but you're going to have to do something with that verse."

He was referring to 1 Corinthians 14:2 (note in brackets is taken from the NLT footnote):

> For if you have the ability to speak in tongues [*in unknown languages*], you will be talking only to God, since people won't be able to understand you. You will be speaking by the power of the Spirit, but it will all be mysterious. (1 Corinthians 14:2 NLT)

I felt defensive because I used to make fun of people who "spoke in tongues." But there it was in the Bible—and written by the apostle Paul, our apostle for today and the apostle for all believers since the moment Jesus struck him blind on the road to Damascus.

So, I knew I would have to do something with that verse. Believe it or reject it. Believe God's Word or reject God's Word. I couldn't just simply ignore it or pretend it didn't exist.

You, too, will need to decide what to do with this verse.

Nowhere in the Bible are we told that this verse isn't for today. *Nowhere.* Including in 1 Corinthians nor anywhere else in Paul's writings.

Some say that 1 Corinthians 13 tells us that tongues have passed away. Let's see if that's what it really says:

> Love never fails; but if there are gifts of prophecy, they will be done away with; if there are tongues, they will cease; if there is knowledge, it will be done away with. For we know in part and prophesy in part; but when the perfect comes, the partial will be done away with. (1 Corinthians 13:8-10)

The verse clearly tells us that gifts of prophecy, tongues, and knowledge *will be* done away with. And this will happen at a future time, when the perfect comes.

According to this verse, if tongues have ceased, then all knowledge has also passed away. But we know this isn't true. Human knowledge continues to advance at a rapid pace. Some individuals and denominations also claim "the perfect" to come is the Bible, specifically the King James Bible (KJB). The King James Bible is *not* the perfect referenced in this verse, that can only be Jesus Christ.

This verse clearly tells us that tongues, prophecy, and knowledge will not pass away until Jesus Christ returns to earth a second time.

Further, tongues and prophecy are gifts. God has never given a gift to believers and then taken it back:

> For the gifts and the calling of God are irrevocable. (Romans 11:29)

God has not revoked this gift of speaking to Him in the Spirit. It is just as available for believers today in the twenty-first century as it was in the first century. Nothing has changed this biblical truth.

Very early in my Christian walk, I made the decision to believe all of God's Word. Every letter and syllable of it. Whether I had read it or not, understood it or not, liked it or not. It was God's Word, after all, so who was I to disagree with the creator of all things?

I learned the very hard way, though, that to know *what* I believed required reading and studying God's Word for myself, not just sitting in church believing everything I heard—or, worse, trusting that I was getting the full truth and that nothing was being withheld from me.

As Christians—followers of Jesus Christ—we all need to believe the Word of God. Every letter and syllable of it. We cannot call ourselves Christians, then pick and choose the verses we like and agree with while rejecting the ones we don't.

We are not the author of scripture; God is. We either believe Him or we don't. We either believe Jesus or we don't. Remember, *He is the Word made flesh*:

> And the Word became flesh, and dwelt among us; and we saw His glory, glory as of the only Son from the Father, full of grace and truth. (John 1:14)

I continue to believe the Word of God without hesitation even as I dig deeper and deeper to uncover more of His truths. I still struggle and wrestle with parts of scripture, but I don't wrestle to win an argument with God or to prove I'm right and He's wrong. I don't wrestle so I can justify my own fleshly opinions. I wrestle to learn, to understand, to know truth—God's truth—the only truth that exists.

That verse, 1 Corinthians 14:2, was staring at me. And, yes, I was going to have to do something with it. Believe it or reject it.

I chose to believe it. I chose to believe God.

At the end of that sermon, the pastor said he was going to lead the congregation in receiving the baptism in the Holy Spirit if they chose to do so.

I didn't hesitate.

I didn't know what I was getting myself into, but I desperately wanted more of God, and that pastor had proven to me that the Holy Spirit *is* God, so I wanted more of Him as well.

There I was, sitting in my living room all by myself, watching a seven-year-old sermon on TV, begging for more of God. More of Jesus. For Him to be more real to me.

So, I stood up all by my lonesome and repeated the pastor's words. I asked Jesus to baptize me in the Holy Spirit.

I immediately felt waves flood over my body from the top of my head down to the soles of my feet. It was real. Very real. Just as real as when my heart jumped in the moment of my salvation way back in 1981.

To be honest, knowing now that I had lived those thirty-six years without the power of the Holy Spirit and without a deeper understanding of scripture felt truly disappointing and frustrating. I was a bit upset. It was like I had lost something of value. Like something had been taken from me. That feeling of disappointment and loss is what motivated me to write this book.

My desire is that you fully understand what Jesus did for you on the cross and experience the baptism in the Holy Spirit. I also hope you learn the importance of searching and studying scripture for yourself—discovering what God's Word actually says versus simply trusting everything you hear in a sermon or see in a social media post or read in a book.

∽

One last thought: Although this book is titled *Evangelicals Are Powerless*, it isn't solely about or for evangelicals. And the title is certainly not meant to denigrate or judge anyone in any way. That is not my intent nor my heart.

Rather, I experienced evangelical churches firsthand for over thirty years and understand them, and thus the title merely reflects my experience and a point of reference for discussing salvation and baptisms, especially baptism in the Holy Spirit. You could easily replace the word "evangelicals" with Baptists or Methodists or any denomination, church, or individual that does not believe in Spirit baptism or has not heard of it or experienced it.

So, it is simply a title. You can certainly be from any Christian church or denomination to read and benefit from this book. More importantly, you can be from *any* Christian church or denomination to receive the baptism in the Holy Spirit!

The only prerequisite for Spirit baptism is that you be truly saved. In 1 Corinthians 15, the apostle Paul recorded the gospel for us today, which we are to believe for the forgiveness of our sins and eternal salvation:

> Let me now remind you, dear brothers and sisters, of the Good News I preached to you before. You welcomed it then, and you still stand firm in it. **It is this Good News that saves you** if you continue to believe the message I told you—unless, of course, you believed something that was never true in the first place. I passed on to you what was most important and what had also been passed on to me. **Christ died for our sins, just as the Scriptures said. He was buried, and he was raised from the dead on the third day, just as the Scriptures said.** (1 Corinthians 15:1-4 NLT)

I spent thirty-six years as a Christian with the Holy Spirit dwelling *in* me, but without His power *upon* me. As I already mentioned, I even ridiculed those who believed in speaking in tongues, even though I had never even heard of baptism in the Holy Spirit or taken the time to study 1 Corinthians 12–14 for myself.

I have now lived eight years *with* the power of the Holy Spirit. I have personally experienced speaking in tongues without even trying—the Holy Spirit speaking (praying) for me with zero effort on my part. And I have had other supernatural experiences as a direct result of my baptism in the Holy Spirit, including word of wisdom, word of knowledge, distinguishing of spirits, and more.

Evangelicals miss or even outright ignore the power of the Holy Spirit to their own detriment—and to the detriment of the Body of Christ and nonbelievers around them.

Don't neglect the ministry and work of the Holy Spirit. From the moment of salvation, He dwells in all believers to sanctify us, convict us away from sin and toward righteousness, and to produce His fruit in us and through us. *But He also works His gifts of power through those baptized in Him— power to witness and build up the Body of Christ.*

So, set your doubts and unbelief aside. Pray and ask God for wisdom and discernment. Then read this book. Search and study the scriptures to determine *for yourself* whether the Holy Spirit baptism aligns with the Word of God or not.

And, finally, I pray that you will open your heart and mind and spirit to receiving this baptism. Seek to experience it for yourself before rejecting it:

> Do not quench the Spirit, do not utterly reject prophecies, but examine everything; hold firmly to that which is good. (1 Thessalonians 5:19-21)

Thank you for reading this book. It was such a blessing and joy to write, and I pray that it's a blessing and joy for you to read as well.

May God richly bless you as you learn more about Him, His Son, His Holy Spirit, and Their precious Word.

~ John

Introduction

WITH THIS BOOK, I have labored to provide a solid scriptural foundation so you can see for yourself what Jesus accomplished on the cross and that every believer in Him can and should experience three baptisms: salvation, water, and Spirit.

Along the way, I'll open the scriptures up more clearly for you. I promise that you'll see God, Jesus, the Holy Spirit, the disciples, the Old Testament, and the New Testament with greater clarity and understanding.

Prior to diving into the three baptisms of believers in Chapter 7, though, we'll first lay some biblical foundations for salvation (Chapter 1), baptisms in the Old Testament (Chapter 2), the person and work of the Holy Spirit (Chapter 3), and the importance of the book of Acts (Chapter 4).

Chapters 5–7 serve as the core of the book by looking at the three baptisms of Jesus (Chapter 5), His disciples (Chapter 6), and believers today (Chapter 7).

The final three chapters will provide details on how to *biblically* receive salvation (Chapter 8), water baptism (Chapter 9), and the baptism in the Holy Spirit (Chapter 10).

Bible Translations Used

My favorite Bible translation is the New American Standard Bible (NASB). I like the King James Version, but the NASB is as accurate but easier to read. So, most of the scripture verses in this book come from the NASB 2020 edition. Where an NASB verse is not as clear, I use the more straightforward wording of the New Living Translation (NLT).

Be sure to check the verses I include against your version of choice.

Reading Order

You can read this book in any order you wish. It is not necessary to read from front to back. However, I do recommend going front to back for those who are newer in their faith or who don't have a good understanding of scripture, especially regarding salvation and baptisms. It's your choice, though. Feel free to pick and choose the chapters that interest you and dig right into them in any order. You will learn and be blessed in whatever order you choose.

As you'll soon see, *Evangelicals Are Powerless* contains a lot of scripture content. It might seem complicated in parts but take your time to read and understand ideas that are new to you. Once you see the first couple "truths" you've never seen before, other truths will begin to fall into place more easily.

I do repeat important concepts throughout the book—for two reasons: 1) If you read the chapters out of order, you're less likely to miss something important. 2) Repetition will help you more quickly learn and grasp the biblical concepts being presented.

Five Key Points

Finally, here are five key biblical truths I hope you take from this book:

1. Salvation is by belief only, not by any works or by any words or prayers. And our gospel for today is what Jesus revealed to the apostle Paul and what Paul later wrote in 1 Corinthians 15:1-4.
2. All believers today can and should experience three baptisms.
3. There is a clear scriptural difference between being indwelled with the Holy Spirit and being filled with the Holy Spirit—having Him come upon a believer with power. *Indwelling* occurs immediately at salvation (conversion), whereas *the power* comes at a separate event called the baptism in (or with) the Holy Spirit.
4. Jesus experienced three baptisms, as did the disciples, the apostle Paul, and many other believers in those days, then millions upon millions since the Day of Pentecost in AD 30.
5. Do not just believe everything any pastor, preacher, teacher, or author says (including me!). Through this book, you will discover that you have not been taught the full truth of God's Word. Read and study the scriptures to discover God's truth for yourself:

Now these people [Bereans] were more noble-minded than those in Thessalonica, for they received the word with great eagerness, examining the Scriptures daily to see whether these things were so. (Acts 17:11)

FOUNDATION CHAPTERS

1
The Truth About Salvation

My Salvation Experience

I DIDN'T GROW up attending church. My mom was raised Catholic but didn't practice. My dad was heathen, and he did practice. I was nineteen in 1981 and in my second year of college. In November of that year, a friend invited me to his church (evangelical, nondenominational). Over the following weeks, I heard the message of salvation for the first time and desperately wanted what I was hearing. On December 15, 1981, I excitedly gave my life to Jesus. I was baptized in water a few weeks later.

As I prayed those words of salvation and freedom in Christ, my heart leaped for joy. I felt it. I still remember the feeling even today. It was such a beautiful moment in my life, one that I have never regretted or questioned in any way over the last forty-plus years.

Fast-forward nearly thirty-six years to May 17, 2017. As I touched on in the Preface, I was baptized in the Holy Spirit that day—*within minutes* of first learning about it.

I was watching a sermon series on a Christian cable network. The preacher was doing a deep dive into the person and work of the Holy Spirit, a topic I knew little to nothing about.

The sermon was different than any I had heard. The pastor wasn't just telling me how to live my Christian life based on a parable or simple Bible story or verse or two. He was teaching the Word of God. I didn't have to just trust what he said, because I could follow along in scripture as he connected *many* verses from the Old and New Testaments. I could hear and read and understand for myself that he was teaching the gospel truth. Gospel truth that I had *never* heard before!

Now, you might be laughing at me, especially if you're used to this kind of preaching. But I promise you, most believers today are *not* taught the Word of God from the pulpit. Instead, many pastors simply seek to entertain their congregations or give basic messages about how to live a better Christian life or how to "live your best life now." They may say something like, "You can live a good Christian life by slaying your giants like David did, being a faithful friend like Ruth, or being a kind neighbor like the good Samaritan." But the Bible holds such deeper revelations than these surface-level teachings—deeper meanings that grow our understanding of God, Jesus, the Holy Spirit, and our faith.

And not only do we receive superficial teachings today, but incorrect teachings as well.

For nearly four decades, I repented for every new sin, both big and small, before I learned the truth about repentance and what Christ *actually* accomplished on the cross and what He meant by His final words, "It is finished."

I'd also been taught that all that crazy stuff in the Bible about prophecy and tongues and the power of the Holy Spirit had been done away with—that God stopped it after the apostles Paul and John died.

As well, I was taught that once I'd been saved and baptized in water, I was fully equipped to lead a good Christian life. I just needed to work hard *not to sin*, and then, when I died, I'd go to heaven. After all, I was taught that even though I was saved, people who sin still go to hell—and the only way to not end up in hell was to be saved *and* not sin. But if you did sin, you had to repent.

None of this is biblical, though. None of it.

No believer should spend decades not understanding the truth of scripture and living life without that truth, without the foundation for greater faith, and without the power of God in their life.

Today, though, there is little to no effort in the pulpits to expose the truth of scripture—the good, the bad, the ugly, as well as the confusing, shocking, and inexplicable.

I see very little effort to explain and connect Genesis to Revelation, to explain that David was a type of Christ, or how Ruth and Boaz connect so beautifully to Jesus in the book of Revelation, or why the action of the good Samaritan was so shocking (Luke 10:25-37). Or, even more critical, how Jesus *already* paid the price for all my sins—past, present, and future—and that I simply needed to believe versus living each day full of guilt and shame, repenting and confessing my sins every fifteen minutes.

Jesus died on the cross so that we could be *forever* forgiven, *forever* righteous in God's eyes, and *not* have to carry the burden of sin any longer:

> Yet we know that a person is made right with God by faith in Jesus Christ, not by obeying the law. And we have believed in Christ Jesus, so that we might be made right with God because of our faith in Christ, not because we have obeyed the law. For no one will ever be made right with God by obeying the law. (Galatians 2:16 NLT)

In addition to a lack of understanding the gospel that saves today and what Jesus accomplished on the cross, the aspect of preaching and teaching that disappoints me just as much is lack of teaching on the Holy Spirit. He was barely a whisper in the evangelical churches I attended. He was ignored. His power was ignored. His gifts dismissed as dead and gone. This lack of understanding of the Holy Spirit continues in the overwhelming majority of churches and denominations today.

Salvation Is Free

We don't need to do *anything* to receive salvation. We just need to believe. Nor do we need to continue working on our salvation once we've believed, as if we need to *keep* ourselves saved by our works. We don't because we can't. That would be like saying, "Jesus, thank You for dying on the cross for me, but it wasn't enough. I'll take it from here."

If you are working hard to stay saved, you missed the point of the cross. You've missed the point of Jesus. You've missed what Jesus already accomplished for you. You are free in Christ, not bound to works—including the works of confession and continually seeking forgiveness for your sins.

I've known evangelicals and other Christians who spend their lives pointing out the sin of others while working hard themselves not to sin. This is not biblical. These individuals don't want others to be free because *they're* not free. They are held back by their own sin, so they hold back other believers as well. They don't really believe that Jesus died to take away their sins. Instead, they have chained themselves to the law. They allow themselves to be continually "punished"—thereby justifying the punishment of others—because they themselves are not forgiven and free in Christ. For them, Christ wasn't punished enough, so they will continue their own punishment for their sins.

Believers don't need to work hard at "not sinning." When we truly believe and receive what Christ did for us on the cross, we die to sin. Forever. We are placed in Christ. We also receive the Holy Spirit to guide us and help us to continually shed acts of sin from our lives.

So, while true believers still sin, we aren't slaves to sin as we were before Christ. We are set free from that bondage. With our eyes fixed on Jesus and with the Holy Spirit in us, we now have the *spiritual power* to look away and walk away from sin.

Sin was always there with us before, though. Tantalizing us. Offering us all kinds of pleasures to satisfy our cravings. Soliciting us to step into tempting spaces and do things we knew not to do. But we didn't have anything, or anyone, to rescue us, to pull us away from those deadly flames, except our own weak human soul. Believers in Jesus Christ, however, are free from sin:

> Don't you realize that you become the slave of whatever you choose to obey? You can be a slave to sin, which leads to death, or you can choose to obey God,

> which leads to righteous living. Thank God! Once you were slaves of sin, but now you wholeheartedly obey this teaching we have given you. Now you are free from your slavery to sin, and you have become slaves to righteous living. (Romans 6:16-18)

Four scripture passages from Paul's letters show the flow of salvation and freedom from sin we have in Christ Jesus.

First, Paul gave us a very clear definition of the Good News that saves today—the gospel message that He received from Jesus—stating exactly what we need to *believe* to be saved:

> Let me now remind you, dear brothers and sisters, of the Good News I preached to you before. You welcomed it then, and you still stand firm in it. It is this Good News that saves you if you continue to believe the message I told you—unless, of course, you believed something that was never true in the first place. **I passed on to you what was most important and what had also been passed on to me. Christ died for our sins, just as the Scriptures said. He was buried, and he was raised from the dead on the third day, just as the Scriptures said.** (1 Corinthians 15:1-4 NLT)

Second, we receive our salvation the exact moment we believe—before we even say a word. There is nothing else we can do, nothing we can say, to be more saved. Also, in that moment, the Holy Spirit baptizes us into the Body of Christ, and He enters us to dwell in us:

> For by one Spirit we were all baptized into one body, whether Jews or Greeks, whether slaves or free, and we were all made to drink of one Spirit. (1 Corinthians 12:13)

Next, we are also sealed by the Holy Spirit to live out eternity in heaven:

> In Him, you also, after listening to the message of truth, the gospel of your salvation—having also believed, you were sealed in Him with the Holy Spirit of the promise. (Ephesians 1:13)

And finally, since we believe *in our heart* what Jesus did for us on the cross, we are a new creation *in Christ*:

> Therefore if anyone is in Christ, this person is a new creation; the old things passed away; behold, new things have come. (2 Corinthians 5:17)

This is the very definition of being a "Christian"—we are "*in Christ.*"

We aren't a Christian because of anything we do or how we behave. We are a Christian because of *what* we believe—that Jesus Christ died for our sins, was buried, and rose from the dead three days later. That's it. Nothing more.

How we behave *after salvation* should reveal that we are a Christian, that Jesus has circumcised our heart and made us a new creation.

No one can be saved or go to heaven based on anything they do, including:

- going to church
- being baptized
- reading the Bible
- praying
- saying a prayer of salvation
- tithing/giving
- being good
- repenting
- confessing sins
- following the Ten Commandments

None of these actions save anyone today.

As we'll see in later chapters, repentance and water baptism were required for Jews during Jesus's earthly ministry. Soon afterward, God sent the apostle Paul to be the apostle to the Gentiles (that's you and me). We are to follow Paul's ministry, which he received *directly from Jesus*.

We are not to follow Jesus's earthly ministry. That is where most preachers and teachers do not understand the Bible, so they preach and teach the wrong gospel. This confuses people and makes scripture difficult to understand. Worse yet, it can leave people believing they are saved and sealed for eternity when they may not be.

Believe and trust in what Jesus has already done for you, not in anything you have done or are doing.

God did not intend for us to live out this faith journey on our own by our own human efforts, always striving hard to not sin. We are simply too weak and powerless. The sooner we accept this and understand Christ's finished work on the cross, the sooner all believers will live a richer, more meaningful, more powerful Christian life.

Similarly, after Jesus ascended to heaven, He did not leave His disciples alone. He hasn't left us alone either. He did not intend for them or us to be apostles, prophets, evangelists, pastors and teachers (Ephesians 4:11-12) or to perform miracles and build the church alone. We simply can't do it. We are human. They were human also. We are all weak and powerless on our own. The disciples grieved the idea of Jesus departing because He made things happen, because He was their power. He told them:

> But now I am going to Him who sent Me; and none of you asks Me, "Where are You going?" But because I have said these things to you, grief has filled your heart. But I tell you the truth: it is to your advantage that I am leaving; for if I do not leave, the Helper will not come to you; but if I go, I will send Him to you. (John 16:5-7)

God sent the Holy Spirit to the disciples *and to you and me*! It is this same Holy Spirit that brought Jesus the supernatural power He carried throughout His earthly ministry. There is not another "Holy Spirit" or source of God's power on earth.

You and I need this same power to live out our Christian walk. We cannot do it alone. It's the Holy Spirit who gives us power to be witnesses for Jesus, to build up other believers, to build up the Body of Christ.

As Andrew Wommack often says: "The Christian life isn't just hard to live; it's impossible to live."

Why is it impossible to live a Christian life?

> For all have sinned and fall short of the glory of God. (Romans 3:23)

There is no getting around the fact that we have all sinned and we live in a sin-filled world. No one will ever meet God's standard. And it's not just that we've all sinned; it's that we are all *sinners*. It is impossible for us to *not* sin. But then, God stepped in:

> God's law was given so that all people could see how sinful they were. But as people sinned more and more, God's wonderful grace became more abundant. (Romans 5:20 NLT)

His grace is so expansive and encompassing, it covers every one of *my* sins, it covers every one of *your* sins, and it covers *every* sin of *every* human who has ever lived. And that grace came in the form of Jesus, specifically His blood shed for us on that cross on Calvary.

God didn't give the Ten Commandments to Moses and the Israelites (really to all humans) so we could know how to live a righteous life by our own efforts, so we could know "God's righteous rules," what we can do and what we cannot do.

No. This is not biblical.

God gave the law so we could know for certain that we *are* sinners. *Everyone* born of a woman is a sinner. *We all* have fallen infinitely short of God's holy and righteous standard. The law simply lets us know what His standard is, even though no one could ever achieve that standard. Well, no one, except *the* One—Jesus.

So, the law clearly reveals to us that we are sinners in need of a Savior. Jesus Christ is the *only* way we are made perfect, sinless, holy, and righteous in God's eyes.

We need His righteousness because God does not allow sin in heaven. The *only* way you and I can gain entrance, then, is through the blood of His Son. Christ's blood became a covering for the sins of the whole world. The only sinless, perfect person who ever lived chose to die on a cross to pay the price for your sins and for mine. Every one of our sins. The sinless took the place of the sinful. The lone innocent man took the place of the guilty masses.

Jesus not only took the place of Barabbas physically on the center cross, but He took *our* place as well. As a result, we get to stand before God on judgment day fully innocent, fully spotless, fully sinless because Jesus shed His blood for us:

> But He was pierced for our offenses,
> He was crushed for our wrongdoings;
> The punishment for our well-being was laid upon him,
> And by His wounds we are healed.
> All of us, like sheep, have gone astray,
> Each of us has turned to his own way;
> But the LORD has caused the wrongdoing of us all
> To fall on Him. (Isaiah 53:5-6)

There is no life in the law, only death and slavery to sin. There is also no life in striving hard to *not* sin. It doesn't work. I can't save myself. You can't save yourself. There is only death in the law. Spiritual death first, then eternal.

Life can only be found in Jesus Christ. But as Paul tells us, life in Christ is available only by dying to the law:

> He has enabled us to be ministers of his new covenant. This is a covenant not of written laws, but of the Spirit. The old written covenant ends in death; but under the new covenant, the Spirit gives life. (2 Corinthians 3:6 NLT)

> But now we have been released from the law, for we died to it and are no longer captive to its power. Now we can serve God, not in the old way of obeying the letter of the law, but in the new way of living in the Spirit. (Romans 7:6 NLT)

When we truly live free in Christ we no longer need to work to maintain our salvation—it is assured—we cannot lose it. Continuing to follow the law (works-based salvation) does not bring freedom but more bondage. It forces us to focus on ourselves to ensure we "stay saved." Living free in Christ allows us to confidently focus on serving God and on the salvation of others since ours is already sealed for eternity.

And lest you think these passages give us an excuse to no longer follow the law and therefore provide a license to sin, check out these verses:

> What shall we say then? Are we to continue in sin so that grace may increase? Far from it! How shall we who died to sin still live in it? (Romans 6:1-2)
>
> Owe nothing to anyone except to love one another; for the one who loves his neighbor has fulfilled the Law. For this, "You shall not commit adultery, You shall not murder, You shall not steal, You shall not covet," and if there is any other commandment, it is summed up in this saying, "You shall love your neighbor as yourself." Love does no wrong to a neighbor; therefore love is the fulfillment of the Law. (Romans 13:8-10)

Jesus did not come to get rid of the law but to fulfill it through His death on the cross. We follow the letter of the law by loving God the Father (Commandments 1-4) and our neighbors (Commandments 5-10).

Does the Holy Spirit Have You?

Now, if you are saved, you have the Holy Spirit dwelling in you. *But... does the Holy Spirit have you?*

That is the real essence of this book. I want you to see that without the baptism in the Holy Spirit, you and I are spiritually powerless.

Don't misunderstand me: God, Jesus, and the Holy Spirit are still wholly all-powerful. They can and do operate supernaturally without us. They do not need our help to save people, to heal, to perform miracles, or to accomplish their will.

God does, however, *want to partner with us!* He desires to be in relationship with us, to work in us and through us to achieve His will, including by supernatural means. He also desires for us to grow spiritually. He desires to teach us, transform us, perfect us, and show us that we need Him and His power way more than He needs us and our feeble human nature.

One final point: Many have the mistaken idea that believers already have the power of the Holy Spirit. That we receive *all* of Him at our moment of salvation. And that there is nothing more to receive.

This is not biblical!

This falsehood produces weak Christians and a weak Body of Christ.

If you believe this, then you've been misled just like I was. There is more of the Holy Spirit waiting for you—much more. Read on and I will prove it to you.

If you are truly saved, then the Holy Spirit is dwelling within you, and He's been there from the moment of your salvation. Read 1 Corinthians 12:13 again:

> For by one Spirit we were all baptized into one body, whether Jews or Greeks, whether slaves or free, and we were all made to drink of one Spirit.

But your salvation baptism experience did not include the Holy Spirit coming *upon you with power* (Acts 1:8). Spirit baptism is a fully separate event from salvation, though it can happen any time after salvation. That could be a few seconds after, a few minutes, hours, days, weeks, even years, or, in my case (unfortunately), decades later.

First Corinthians 12:13 reveals two special things that happen at our conversion: First, the *Holy Spirit baptizes* us into the Body of Christ. (Welcome to the family!) Second, we are "made to drink of one Spirit." This means we receive the Holy Spirit into our life, to dwell in us, specifically into our heart:

> Don't you realize that your body is the temple of the Holy Spirit, who lives in you and was given to you by God? You do not belong to yourself, for God bought you with a high price. So you must honor God with your body. (1 Corinthians 6:19-20 NLT)

> It is God who enables us, along with you, to stand firm for Christ. He has commissioned us, and he has identified us as his own by placing the Holy Spirit in our hearts as the first installment that guarantees everything he has promised us. (2 Corinthians 1:21-22 NLT)

> And because we are his children, God has sent the Spirit of his Son into our hearts, prompting us to call out, "Abba, Father." (Galatians 4:6 NLT)

The work of the Holy Spirit within us is to sanctify us. To set us apart as holy for the work of God, and to continue that sanctification process for the remainder of our life. Through this sanctification process, the Holy Spirit continually makes us more holy, righteous, and obedient.

But wait, there's a third special thing that happens during conversion! Because you *believed* in your heart that Jesus died for you, that He bore your sins on the cross (your past, present, and future sins), and that He was then buried and three days later rose again (1 Corinthians 15:1-4), *you were also sealed in Christ* to live for the remainder of eternity with Him in heaven.

Being sealed means that no one can take your salvation away from you. No one can steal your place in heaven. Not even Satan. Trust that your eternal heavenly home is secure in Christ, sealed with the Holy Spirit, a gift from the Father, a gift He will never take back.

Here is that promise in Ephesians once again:

> In Him, you also, after listening to the message of truth, the gospel of your salvation—having also believed, you were sealed in Him with the Holy Spirit of the promise. (Ephesians 1:13)

You were sealed simply by believing. Nothing more. No prayer. No words. No works. Christ did it all for you already. You just need to believe.

With all this in mind, let's now look at the fascinating history of baptisms in the Old Testament.

2

The Truth About Water Baptism

The New Covenant Brings a New Baptism

JOHN THE BAPTIST was an Old Testament prophet. He came preaching and prophesying in the style of other Old Testament prophets. Jesus even compared him to Elijah:

> "But I say to you that Elijah already came, and they did not recognize him, but did to him whatever they wanted. So also the Son of Man is going to suffer at their hands." Then the disciples understood that He had spoken to them about John the Baptist. (Matthew 17:12-13)

John the Baptist's ministry, while certainly recorded in the New Testament, actually took place during the Old Testament period. The old covenant (the law and the prophets) was still in effect throughout Jesus's life and ministry, ending only with His death on the cross. Through Christ's death, God ushered in a new covenant for Israel, one that would later be extended to Gentiles as well:

> And when He had taken a cup and given thanks, He said, "Take this and share it among yourselves; for I say to you, I will not drink of the fruit of the vine from now on until the kingdom of God comes." And when He had taken some bread and given thanks, He broke it and gave it to them, saying, "This is My body, which is being given for you; do this in remembrance of Me." And in the same way He took the cup after they had eaten, saying, "This cup, which is poured out for you, is the new covenant in My blood." (Luke 22:17-20)

This new covenant is not anchored in the physical but the spiritual. Not carved in stone tablets but into the body of Jesus. Not of physical circumcision of the body but of spiritual circumcision of the heart. Not of the earthly realm but of the spiritual realm. And not where we're washed in water to *symbolize* a physical cleansing from sin but where we're washed in the blood of Jesus, symbolizing a spiritual cleansing from sin.

Jesus's baptism is one of the most iconic events in the Bible. All four writers of the gospels include the event in their book. Here is how the apostle John described the moment John the Baptist saw Jesus approaching him:

> The next day John saw Jesus coming toward him and said, "Look! The Lamb of God who takes away the sin of the world! He is the one I was talking about when I said, 'A man is coming after me who is far greater than I am, for he existed long before me.' I did not

recognize him as the Messiah, but I have been baptizing with water so that he might be revealed to Israel." (John 1:29-31 NLT)

To be clear, John the Baptist didn't invent baptisms, nor did he even initiate them. God did. John was simply fulfilling God's call on his life to prepare the hearts of the Jewish people for their long-awaited Messiah. He did this by preaching a message of repentance and baptism:

> Now in those days John the Baptist came, preaching in the wilderness of Judea, saying, "Repent, for the kingdom of heaven is at hand." (Matthew 3:1-2)

> And he came into all the region around the Jordan, preaching a baptism of repentance for the forgiveness of sins. (Luke 3:3)

Jesus would soon preach this same message—the Good News ("gospel") that the kingdom of God (or kingdom of heaven) had arrived, which comes through Jesus Christ:

> Now after John was taken into custody, Jesus came into Galilee, preaching the gospel of God, and saying, "The time is fulfilled, and the kingdom of God is at hand; repent and believe in the gospel." (Mark 1:14-15)

Now God had instituted water immersion for ritual cleansing some fifteen hundred years prior through Moses when the Israelites wandered in the wilderness complaining and wishing they were back in slavery in Egypt.

In ancient Hebrew, a ritual cleansing was called a *miqveh* or *mikveh*. The word *mikveh* can have multiple meanings, including a "gathering together (of water)," "pond," or "pool." It can also mean "hope."

Further, the Hebrew word for immersion is *tevilah*. It equates to the English word "baptism," which itself comes directly from the Koine Greek word *baptizo*.

Together, the words *mikveh* and *tevilah* refer to the biblical act of immersing oneself in a natural *living* water source (think river or stream) for the ritual cleansing of sin. The Israelites later built man-made *mikveh* baths but still filled them from streams or rivers to ensure cleansings continued in living water. (A *mikveh* was never used for cleaning or bathing to remove dirt from the body.)

Tabernacle / Temple Cleansings

A ritual cleansing could be with the full body, the hands and feet alone, or just the hands. Among the many purposes of ritual cleansings mentioned in the book of Leviticus, priests especially needed to cleanse themselves prior to entering the Holy Place and the Most Holy Place inside the tabernacle (later the permanent temple). To meet with God inside the Most Holy Place, one had to be clean of sin, hence the *mikveh*.

God hasn't changed. There can be no sin in His presence, including in heaven. For *anyone* to enter heaven, they must be sinless. We are only sinless through Christ's blood sacrifice on the cross. Christ, therefore, became our ritual cleansing.

In the book of Exodus, God instructed Moses to craft a small water basin (laver) out of bronze for priests to ritually cleanse their hands and feet. The basin sat inside the courtyard of the tabernacle, just past the altar of burnt offering and before the entrance to the Holy Place. (See Exhibit 1.) The Holy Place itself contained other tabernacle elements, including the altar of incense. The ark of the covenant, which contained the stone tablets, sat inside the Most Holy Place:

> Then the LORD spoke to Moses, saying, "You shall also make a basin of bronze, with its base of bronze, for washing; and you shall put it between the tent of meeting and the altar, and you shall put water in it. Aaron and his sons shall wash their hands and their feet from it; when they enter the tent of meeting, they shall wash with water, so that they do not die; or when they approach the altar to minister, by offering up in smoke a fire sacrifice to the LORD. So they shall wash their hands and their feet, so that they do not die; and it shall be a permanent statute for them, for Aaron and his descendants throughout their generations." (Exodus 30:17-21)

When King Solomon later built the first permanent temple in Jerusalem, he had a much larger basin (or "Sea") built. It was still circular but measured fifteen feet in diameter (1 Kings 7:23).

One time each year on the Day of Atonement (Yom Kippur), the high priest (who served as mediator between God and the Israelites) would enter the Most Holy Place in the temple. He would go through the courtyard, enter the Holy Place, and, finally, pass through the veil (or curtain) into the Most Holy Place and the presence of God.

Today, we can enter God's presence solely by believing in the death, burial, and resurrection of Jesus Christ for the forgiveness of our sins. Proof of this rests in the fact that, when Jesus died, the veil at the entrance to the Most Holy Place was torn from top to bottom. It opened the way for us to encounter God directly ourselves without the need to go through a pastor or priest or *any* human:

> And Jesus cried out again with a loud voice, and gave up His spirit. And behold, the veil of the temple was torn in two from top to bottom; and the earth shook and the rocks were split. (Matthew 27:50-51)
>
> Jesus said to him, "I am the way, and the truth, and the life; no one comes to the Father except through Me." (John 14:6)
>
> For there is one God, and one mediator also between God and mankind, the man Christ Jesus. (1 Timothy 2:5)

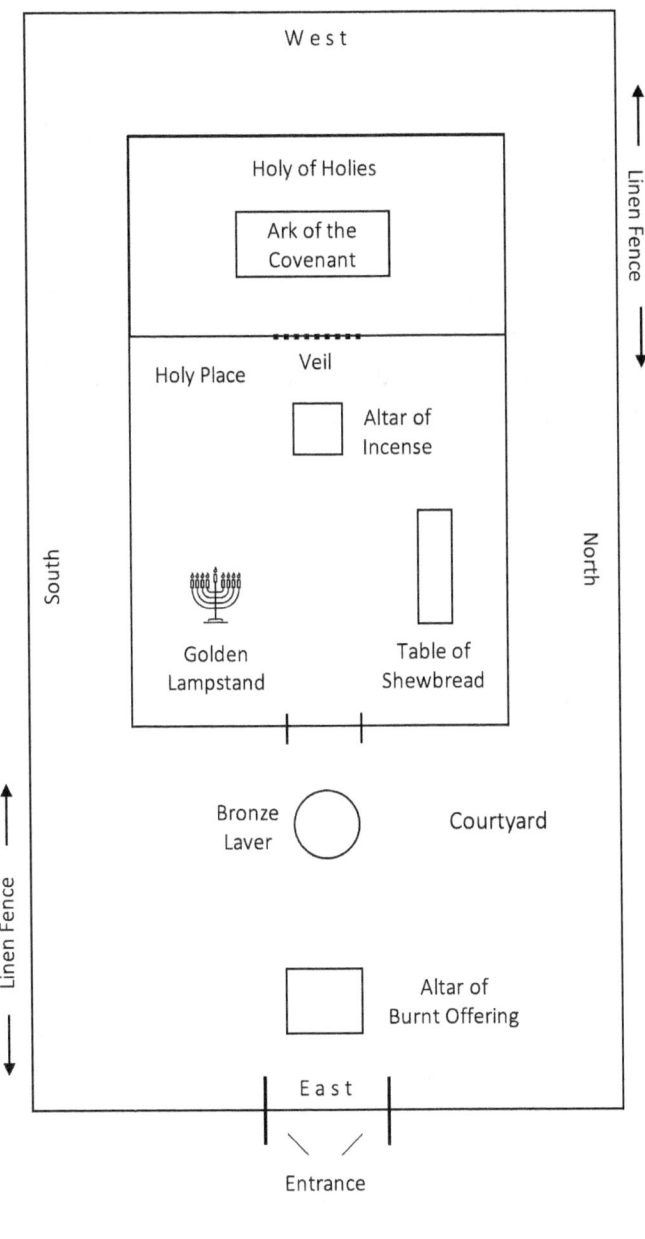

— **Exhibit 1** —

As you can see, water immersions and cleansings have been a very "Jewish" practice since the days of Moses. So, when God sent John the Baptist to the Jewish nation to prepare the way for their Messiah, no one would have questioned the idea of full-body immersion in water for the remittance or spiritual cleansing from sin.

Supernatural Baptisms

Our God is a big, purposeful, and creative God. There is none like Him. We don't need to look beyond the sacrifice of His Son for our salvation to understand just how awesome He is—our new life in His Son is living proof of just how big, purposeful, and creative He is.

God showed up in big ways throughout scripture with baptisms. This is especially true in the Old Testament where He worked in ways only *He* could imagine and accomplish. Here are a few God-sized baptisms (supernatural cleansings) we sometimes overlook.

Noah and the Flood

The story of Noah, the ark, and the global flood is recorded in the book of Genesis 6–9. Peter also mentioned the event in his first epistle:

> Christ suffered for our sins once for all time. He never sinned, but he died for sinners to bring you safely home to God. He suffered physical death, but he was raised to life in the Spirit. So he went and preached to the spirits in prison—those who disobeyed God long ago when God waited patiently while Noah was building his boat. Only eight people were saved from drowning

> in that terrible flood. **And that water is a picture of baptism, which now saves you, not by removing dirt from your body, but as a response to God from a clean conscience. It is effective because of the resurrection of Jesus Christ.** (1 Peter 3:18-21 NLT)

Noah and his family lived for a full year in that ark upon the water. They were "saved through the water," as it says in many other translations. The ark represents Christ as their means of salvation, just as Christ is our means of salvation.

What makes water baptism significant for us today isn't that we're washed in water for our salvation but that it's a *symbolic* washing in the blood of Jesus Christ for the removal of our sins.

And further, those with Noah in the ark were 100 percent reliant on God for their salvation, through *the faith of Noah*. They could not in any way save themselves. (Those who died in the flood did not have the faith required for salvation.) Likewise, today, we are 100 percent reliant on God and His Son for our salvation.

Parting of the Red Sea

Most know the story of God parting the Red Sea so that Moses could lead the Israelites through it on dry ground, thereby escaping the Egyptian army in hot pursuit behind them. But did you know that God parted waters four times in scripture, and that each one is considered a baptism?

God parted:

1. the Red Sea for Moses and the Israelites (Exodus 14:21-22).

2. the Jordan River for Joshua and the Israelites (Joshua 3:14-17).
3. the Jordan River for Elijah and Elisha (2 Kings 2:8-9).
4. the Jordan River for Elisha (2 Kings 2:14).

We'll only touch on the first two events, so be sure to check out the "baptism" events in 2 Kings yourself.

It can be difficult to view the parting of the Red Sea as a baptism, but that is exactly what it was. You don't have to take my word for it, though, as Paul wrote about it:

> For I do not want you to be unaware, brothers and sisters, that our fathers were all under the cloud and they all passed through the sea; and they all were baptized into Moses in the cloud and in the sea. (1 Corinthians 10:1-2)

The writer of Hebrews tells us:

> By faith they passed through the Red Sea as through dry land; and the Egyptians, when they attempted it, were drowned. (Hebrews 11:29)

Moses led the Israelites out of Egypt and, soon after, through the Red Sea. They went into the midst of the water and came out, leaving behind their four hundred years of bondage to slavery. This is a foreshadowing of our own salvation, in which we are baptized into Jesus's death, burial, and resurrection, forever separating us from our bondage to sin.

Our water baptism, then, symbolizes our own death, burial, and resurrection. Just like their immersion in the Red Sea didn't save the Israelites (their faith in God did), water baptism doesn't save us either. We are saved only through faith in the shed blood of Jesus Christ, which happens when we are baptized by the Holy Spirit into the Body of Christ and cleansed by the blood of Christ:

> For by one Spirit we were all baptized into one body, whether Jews or Greeks, whether slaves or free, and we were all made to drink of one Spirit. (1 Corinthians 12:13)

God's parting of the Red Sea foreshadows water baptisms today. Just as God *physically* immersed the Israelites in the water and brought them out, we are immersed in water and then brought out as well, *symbolically* representing the fact that we were forever separated from bondage to sin.

And when God closed the Red Sea behind the Israelites, He wasn't just killing that enemy (because they had no faith); He was showing His chosen nation that they were forever separated and free from their bondage to the Egyptians. He was leading them forward to a new life of freedom and, ultimately, to their Promised Land.

Likewise, living in bondage to sin keeps us separated from God and from living a life of true freedom in Christ. But salvation brings righteousness. It puts us in right standing with God while, at the same time, with our eyes fixed on Jesus, it also keeps us forever separated from the bondage to sin that leads to death—not only spiritual death but a second physical death as well:

> It was for freedom that Christ set us free; therefore keep standing firm and do not be subject again to a yoke of slavery. (Galatians 5:1)

Moses was a type (prophetic symbol) of Christ. He delivered the Israelites from their yoke of slavery just as Christ has delivered us from our own yoke of slavery to sin.

Further, as we saw in 1 Corinthians 10:1-2, the Israelites were baptized into Moses by the cloud (Holy Spirit) and by the sea (water), just as we are baptized into Jesus by the Holy Spirit at our salvation, as well as by water at our water baptism.

Notice, however, that the Israelites weren't spiritually empowered once they came out of the cloud and sea. So, their experience did not include a "baptism in the Holy Spirit." And just like the Israelites, we also aren't spiritually empowered after our salvation and water baptisms. *We need a third baptism—a baptism in (or with) the Holy Spirit.*

This is biblically provable. There is no place in the Old Testament where the Holy Spirit came upon, into, or indwelled anyone permanently. We even see King David cry out to the Lord:

> Do not cast me away from Your presence, And do not take Your Holy Spirit from me. (Psalm 51:11)

As we will learn in Chapter 5, Jesus was the first to receive the baptism with the Holy Spirit. This happened immediately after His water baptism in the Jordan River by John the Baptist. The apostles later also had the Holy Spirit come upon them on the Day of Pentecost, fifty days after Jesus's resurrection.

Joshua at the Jordan River

Moses led the Israelites to the edge of the Promised Land, stopping on the east side of the Jordan River across from Jericho. But God would not allow Moses to lead His people into their land due to his lack of faith at Meribah (Numbers 20:8-13). Instead, God called on Joshua to lead the nation across:

> "And it will come about when the soles of the feet of the priests who carry the ark of the LORD, the Lord of all the earth, rest in the waters of the Jordan, the waters of the Jordan will be cut off, that is, the waters which are flowing down from above; and they will stand in one heap." So when the people set out from their tents to cross the Jordan, with the priests carrying the ark of the covenant before the people, and when those who were carrying the ark came up to the Jordan and the feet of the priests carrying the ark stepped down into the edge of the water (for the Jordan overflows all its banks all the days of harvest), then the waters which were flowing down from above stood and rose up in one heap, a great distance away at Adam, the city that is beside Zarethan; and those which were flowing down toward the sea of the Arabah, the Salt Sea, were completely cut off. So the people crossed opposite Jericho. And the priests who carried the ark of the covenant of the LORD stood firm on dry ground in the middle of the Jordan while all Israel crossed on dry ground, until all the nation had finished crossing the Jordan. (Joshua 3:13-17)

The Israelites were "immersed" in the Jordan River just as they'd been in the Red Sea forty years earlier. Once again, God parted the waters so they could pass through on dry ground.

Crossing the Jordan River took the nation three days. The Jordan River baptism foreshadows John the Baptist's ministry of baptisms in that same river, and the three days of immersion foreshadows Jesus's own immersion in the grave for three days. (More on this in Chapter 5!)

Jonah and the Whale (Great Big Fish)
The prophet Jonah is another type of Christ who experienced a supernatural baptism. His baptism foreshadowed Christ's, but in a unique way.

Here, Jesus confirms for us the sign of Jonah:

> Then some of the scribes and Pharisees said to Him, "Teacher, we want to see a sign from You." But He answered and said to them, "An evil and adulterous generation craves a sign; and so no sign will be given to it except the sign of Jonah the prophet; for just as Jonah was in the stomach of the sea monster for three days and three nights, so will the Son of Man be in the heart of the earth for three days and three nights." (Matthew 12:38-40)

Jonah wasn't just thrown into the sea (immersed in water) as a ritual cleansing for sin (though he did sin against God) but so God could get Jonah's attention and get him back with the program. God wasn't punishing Jonah. God does not punish His children. If you have that belief, release it. God does not punish His children; He teaches us. Sometimes those lessons bring pain and suffering and can feel very much like punishment. Set yourself free from this idea so you can see, understand, and experience the full goodness of God. He isn't just filled with love, joy, grace, mercy, peace, and forgiveness; He *is* love, joy, grace, mercy, peace, and forgiveness. These attributes are part of God's character; they are who He is. He does not and will not withhold these from you. Ever!

But God will carry us into and through trials and tribulations to grow our character, our hope, our faith, and our freedom in Christ:

> And not only this, but we also celebrate in our tribulations, knowing that tribulation brings about perseverance; and perseverance, proven character; and proven character, hope; and hope does not disappoint, because the love of God has been poured out within our hearts through the Holy Spirit who was given to us. (Romans 5:3-5)

> Blessed is a man who perseveres under trial; for once he has been approved, he will receive the crown of life which the Lord has promised to those who love Him. (James 1:12)

God told His prophet Jonah to go and preach to the city of Nineveh (in ancient Assyria—modern Iraq today). It was a pagan city, and the idea of going there caused Jonah to fear. So, he ran in the opposite direction—away from Nineveh and away from God.

As a result, God "cleansed" Jonah of his sin of not obeying His command to go to Nineveh by tossing him into the sea.

He then immersed the prophet into the belly of a great fish for three days and three nights. Jonah finally called out to the Lord in his distress. God rescued him by commanding the fish spit him out onto dry land:

> Then Jonah prayed to the Lord his God from inside the fish. He said,
> "I cried out to the Lord in my great trouble,
> and he answered me.
> I called to you from the land of the dead,
> and Lord, you heard me!
> You threw me into the ocean depths,
> and I sank down to the heart of the sea.
> The mighty waters engulfed me;
> I was buried beneath your wild and stormy waves.
> Then I said, 'O Lord, you have driven me from your presence.
> Yet I will look once more toward your holy Temple.'
> "I sank beneath the waves,
> and the waters closed over me.
> Seaweed wrapped itself around my head.
> I sank down to the very roots of the mountains.
> I was imprisoned in the earth,
> whose gates lock shut forever.
> But you, O Lord my God,
> snatched me from the jaws of death!
> As my life was slipping away,
> I remembered the Lord.
> And my earnest prayer went out to you
> in your holy Temple.
> Those who worship false gods

turn their backs on all God's mercies.
But I will offer sacrifices to you with songs of praise,
and I will fulfill all my vows.
For my salvation comes from the Lord alone."
Then the Lord ordered the fish to spit Jonah out
onto the beach. (Jonah 2:1-10 NLT)

While Jesus experienced a water baptism, He also experienced pain and suffering just like Jonah had. Jonah disobeyed God and deserved his trouble. Jesus did not deserve what He received; you and I deserved it. We are the guilty ones, just like Jonah. But Jesus humbled Himself, became a servant, and took our place on the cross:

> Though he was God, he did not think of equality with God as something to cling to. Instead, he gave up his divine privileges; he took the humble position of a slave and was born as a human being. When he appeared in human form, he humbled himself in obedience to God and died a criminal's death on a cross. (Philippians 2:6-8 NLT)

Somebody needs to pay the price for our sins. Those who do not believe that Jesus bled and died on the cross for their sins will pay the price themselves when they meet Him face to face at the great white throne judgment (Revelation 20:11-15).

Those of us who do believe we are saved by the blood of the Lamb have Jesus to thank for paying the price of our sin on our behalf. That is atonement. In Hebrew, it means "to cover." Jesus covered our sins with His blood. It is also redemption and why He is our Redeemer.

Believers will also be judged one day, but at a different judgment. Jesus will stand in our place and represent us as sinless and righteous before His Father. Because Jesus paid the price for our sins, we will be able to enter heaven and abide in God's presence for the remainder of eternity.

PRAISE GOD!

Noah (and the ark), Moses, Joshua, and Jonah are all a "type" of Christ in that they experienced baptisms that brought about salvation or delivery of people. None of those men were the ultimate deliverer, though. That was God. Those men needed to be saved themselves. They had no choice but to trust God, to put their faith in Him, to fully rely on Him for their salvation.

You and I are in the same situation—the same boat! (Pardon the pun.) We're not in a literal boat, though, watching everyone around us drown or get swallowed up by the sea or by the gulp of a great fish. But our situation is just as deadly. We are in the jaws of sin.

Only God's supernatural provision could save Noah and his family, the Israelites (twice!), and Jonah and everyone in Nineveh. And only God's supernatural provision of His Son nailed to a cross and in the grave for three days can save us from the perils of spiritual death, as well as a second death in the lake of fire.

We serve such an awesome God!

Finally, no discussion of Old Testament baptisms is complete without mentioning Psalm 51. Below are the three most beautiful verses from this psalm relevant to baptisms. These verses reveal King David's deep desire to be clean before God, knowing that He would be faithful to cleanse him (and us) from all sin:

Wash me thoroughly from my guilt
And cleanse me from my sin....
Purify me with hyssop, and I will be clean;
Cleanse me, and I will be whiter than snow....
Create in me a clean heart, God,
And renew a steadfast spirit within me.
(Psalm 51:2, 7, 10)

Now that we have a good understanding of baptisms from the Old Testament, let's have some fun diving into the person, work, and nature of the Holy Spirit!

3

Get to Know the Holy Spirit

God the Holy Spirit

THIS REVIEW OF the Holy Spirit is meant to provide a solid yet basic understanding of His work and role in scripture and in the lives of believers. God's presence dwells in every believer through the person of the Holy Spirit. He is given freely to those who are saved in Christ:

> For by one Spirit we were all baptized into one body, whether Jews or Greeks, whether slaves or free, and we were all made to drink of one Spirit. (1 Corinthians 12:13)

The Holy Spirit is the third person of the Godhead (Trinity). He's not third because He's less important or because He came in third in a popularity contest but because He was third to be revealed in scripture as a person of the Godhead. This occurred near the end of Jesus's earthly ministry when Jesus promised the disciples that, once He ascended, His Father would send another Helper to be with them forever (John 14:16-17; 16:12-15; Acts 1:5-8).

God the Father is the first person of the Trinity revealed in the Bible, Jesus the second, and the Holy Spirit third. It is scripturally correct to say, "God the Father, God the Son, and God the Holy Spirit."

Calling them "persons" does not mean that they are human beings. They are not. It is simply the best word to convey their nature. They each have a mind, emotions, and will, just as we humans do. After all, we are made in the image of God:

> Then God said, "Let Us make mankind in Our image, according to Our likeness." (Genesis 1:26a)

There is just one God. However, God exists in three distinct persons. Each is co-equal and co-eternal (having no beginning and no ending). Nowhere does the Bible teach that there is only one God manifested as just one entity or one person. It also doesn't teach that there is one God who can appear in three different forms. In fact, all three are clearly present and distinct at Jesus's baptism in the Jordan River:

> After He was baptized, Jesus came up immediately from the water; and behold, the heavens were opened, and he saw the Spirit of God descending as a dove and settling on Him, and behold, a voice from the heavens said, "This is My beloved Son, with whom I am well pleased." (Matthew 3:16-17)

Further, Paul distinguished the Three by reminding believers in Ephesus (and therefore us) that we all have direct access to God the Father by the Holy Spirit solely because of Christ's work on the cross:

> Now all of us can come to the Father through the same Holy Spirit because of what Christ has done for us. (Ephesians 2:18 NLT)

The Holy Spirit also existed from the beginning along with God and Jesus:

> In the beginning God created the heavens and the earth. And the earth was a formless and desolate emptiness, and darkness was over the surface of the deep, and the Spirit of God was hovering over the surface of the waters. (Genesis 1:1-2)

Finally, it's important to understand that, as shown in the above verse, the Holy Spirit was *not* a created being. Neither was God Himself (of course), nor was Jesus. All three existed from before anything existed—time, space, or matter:

> In the beginning the Word already existed. The Word was with God, and the Word was God. He existed in the beginning with God. God created everything through him, and nothing was created except through him. (John 1:1-3 NLT)

His Names and Roles

The Holy Spirit carries many different names throughout scripture. Most of these names also describe His many roles.

First, there is no distinction between the name "Holy Spirit" and "Holy Ghost." Their use is solely a matter of tradition or personal preference. Both names are acceptable and biblical.

"Holy Ghost" is found in the King James Version of the Bible, while pretty much every other translation uses "Holy Spirit." The King James Version does use Holy Spirit at times, but predominantly Holy Ghost.

It is acceptable to use the definite article "the" in front of Holy Spirit and Holy Ghost or to omit it. This, too, is a matter of tradition or personal preference—so, Holy Spirit, Holy Ghost, the Holy Spirit, the Holy Ghost are all the same and honor Him.

Other names you'll find in scripture for the Holy Spirit are:

Helper

> I will ask the Father, and He will give you another Helper, so that He may be with you forever. (John 14:16)

> And the Holy Spirit helps us in our weakness. For example, we don't know what God wants us to pray for. But the Holy Spirit prays for us with groanings that cannot be expressed in words. And the Father who knows all hearts knows what the Spirit is saying, for the Spirit pleads for us believers in harmony with God's own will. (Romans 8:26-27 NLT)

Spirit of Truth

The Helper is the Spirit of truth, whom the world cannot receive, because it does not see Him or know Him; but you know Him because He remains with you and will be in you. (John 14:17)

Eternal Spirit

Just think how much more the blood of Christ will purify our consciences from sinful deeds so that we can worship the living God. For by the power of the eternal Spirit, Christ offered himself to God as a perfect sacrifice for our sins. (Hebrews 9:14 NLT)

Spirit of Life

For the law of the Spirit of life in Christ Jesus has set you free from the law of sin and of death. (Romans 8:2)

Spirit of the Father

But when they hand you over, do not worry about how or what you are to say; for what you are to say will be given you in that hour. For it is not you who are speaking, but it is the Spirit of your Father who is speaking in you. (Matthew 10:19-20)

Spirit of the Promise

> In Him, you also, after listening to the message of truth, the gospel of your salvation—having also believed, you were sealed in Him with the Holy Spirit of the promise. (Ephesians 1:13)

The Breath of God That Inspired Scripture

> Above all, you must realize that no prophecy in Scripture ever came from the prophet's own understanding, or from human initiative. No, those prophets were moved by the Holy Spirit, and they spoke from God. (2 Peter 1:20-21 NLT)

Consider also the final words of King David as recounted by the prophet Samuel:

> The Spirit of the LORD spoke through me,
> And His word was on my tongue. (2 Samuel 23:2)

God is the author of His Word—both the written Word and His Son (John 1:1). God breathed out His written Word through the Holy Spirit. The Spirit Himself inspired the written Word into existence through God's chosen prophets (messengers), eventually producing both the Old and New Testaments.

His Personality and Nature

The Holy Spirit is a person. He is not a thing, an energy, a force, or an "it." There are dozens of verses in the Bible that reference the Holy Spirit using the personal pronouns He/Him. Even Jesus refers to the Holy Spirit as "Him":

> But I tell you the truth: it is to your advantage that I am leaving; for if I do not leave, the Helper will not come to you; but if I go, I will send Him to you. (John 16:7)

King David reveals to us that, like God and Jesus, the Holy Spirit is omnipresent (everywhere):

> Where can I go from Your Spirit?
> Or where can I flee from Your presence?
> If I ascend to heaven, You are there;
> If I make my bed in Sheol, behold, You are there.
> If I take up the wings of the dawn,
> If I dwell in the remotest part of the sea,
> Even there Your hand will lead me,
> And Your right hand will take hold of me.
> If I say, "Surely the darkness will overwhelm me,
> And the light around me will be night,"
> Even darkness is not dark to You,
> And the night is as bright as the day.
> Darkness and light are alike to You.
> For You created my innermost parts;
> You wove me in my mother's womb. (Psalm 139:7-13)

He is also omniscient (all-knowing):

> But the Helper, the Holy Spirit whom the Father will send in My name, He will teach you all things, and remind you of all that I said to you. (John 14:26)

> For to us God revealed them through the Spirit; for the Spirit searches all things, even the depths of God. For who among people knows the thoughts of a person except the spirit of the person that is in him? So also the thoughts of God no one knows, except the Spirit of God. (1 Corinthians 2:10–11)

He is omnipotent (all-powerful):

> But if the Spirit of Him who raised Jesus from the dead dwells in you, He who raised Christ Jesus from the dead will also give life to your mortal bodies through His Spirit who dwells in you. (Romans 8:11)

He has feelings:

> Do not grieve the Holy Spirit of God, by whom you were sealed for the day of redemption. (Ephesians 4:30)

> But the fruit of the Spirit is love, joy, peace, patience, kindness, goodness, faithfulness, gentleness, self-control; against such things there is no law. (Galatians 5:22-23)

He can be lied to:

> But Peter said, "Ananias, why has Satan filled your heart to lie to the Holy Spirit and to keep back some of the proceeds of the land?" (Acts 5:3)

He can be resisted:

> You men who are stiff-necked and uncircumcised in heart and ears are always resisting the Holy Spirit; you are doing just as your fathers did. (Acts 7:51)

He has a mind:

> And the Father who knows all hearts knows what the Spirit is saying, for the Spirit pleads for us believers in harmony with God's own will. (Romans 8:27 NLT)

And He speaks:

> Then the Spirit said to Philip, "Go up and join this chariot." (Acts 8:29)

Biblical Symbols of the Holy Spirit

The Holy Spirit is represented throughout scripture by many different symbols and images. We'll look at just five of the more prevalent ones.

Dove

The dove is the most recognized symbol for the Holy Spirit. In the Bible, the dove represents peace, power, and innocence, among other concepts.

The most memorable story of the Holy Spirit represented as a dove occurs after Jesus is baptized in the Jordan River. The Holy Spirit comes upon Him "as a dove," immersing Jesus in power:

> After He was baptized, Jesus came up immediately from the water; and behold, the heavens were opened, and he saw the Spirit of God descending as a dove and settling on Him. (Matthew 3:16)

Notice that the Holy Spirit didn't show up as an actual dove but descended "as a dove" or "like a dove." Whatever form He took in that moment, the Spirit softly flowed down and settled upon Jesus. I always imagine a soft white light gracefully descending, gliding down as if with wings of light spread wide.

Doves were more than just another "two by two" animal Noah loaded into the ark in the story of the flood from Genesis 6–8. Once the waters began to subside, Noah sent out a dove to determine if the waters had dried up enough to expose land. Noah sent the dove out three times. It returned the first time with no resting place for its feet. Upon its second return, it carried a fresh olive leaf in its beak. The dove here symbolizes God's peace and the olive leaf reconciliation following His judgment of mankind. Noah then sent the dove out a third time:

> Then he waited another seven days longer, and sent out the dove; but it did not return to him again. (Genesis 8:12)

Wind

The Old Testament was originally written in ancient Hebrew. The English phrase "Holy Spirit" (or "Holy Ghost") comes directly from the Hebrew words *Ruach HaKodesh*.

Ruach is the Hebrew word for "spirit," "breath," or "wind." *Kodesh* means "holy." Together, we get *Ruach HaKodesh*, or Holy Spirit.

The New Testament was mostly written in Koine Greek. Here, we find the Greek phrase *Hagios Pneuma* (or some form of it). *Hagios* means "holy" and *pneuma* means "wind," "breath," or "air."

This isn't intended to be a study about the Hebrew and Greek phrases for Holy Spirit. I honestly don't have the knowledge or training for that! I simply want to show you that the Hebrew and Greek phrases for Holy Spirit indicate "holy wind," "holy air," or even "holy breath." It's no surprise, then, that the Holy Spirit is often referred to as wind or air or breath throughout scripture:

> The wind blows where it wishes, and you hear the sound of it, but you do not know where it is coming from and where it is going; so is everyone who has been born of the Spirit. (John 3:8)

> And suddenly a noise like a violent rushing wind came from heaven, and it filled the whole house where they were sitting. (Acts 2:2)

Wind is such a perfect word to name *and* describe the Holy Spirit. The word embodies both Him and His work.

For example, wind is powerful, which is the exact purpose of the Holy Spirit: to bring the power of God to earth and fill the lives of believers. Wind moves all around us, just as the Holy Spirit moves all around us and within us. Wind changes and transforms our environment, just as the Holy Spirit changes and transforms us into the image of God:

> So all of us who have had that veil removed can see and reflect the glory of the Lord. And the Lord—who is the Spirit—makes us more and more like him as we are changed into his glorious image. (2 Corinthians 3:18 NLT)

As well, just like the wind, we cannot see the Holy Spirit, but we can see the effects of Him. The wind can also be truly relentless, just as the Holy Spirit is relentless in pursuing us and transforming us.

There is also a never-ending supply of the Holy Spirit and His power, just like there is a never-ending supply of the wind and its power. Finally, just like the wind, the Holy Spirit will show up and overwhelm us with His power when we least expect it.

Fire

Fire is a common symbol throughout the Bible and very often refers directly to the Holy Spirit or His activity. In these instances, we see God's power, presence, guidance (guiding light), and refinement at work through His Spirit.

For example, through God's mighty power, Moses led the Israelites out of Egypt and through the Red Sea. God then led them, *via the Holy Spirit*, by a pillar of cloud by day and pillar of fire by night. Through the guiding presence of the Spirit of God, God the Father led the Israelites farther away from bondage and closer to Him and the land and abundant life He promised Abraham. This is exactly what God does for us through His Spirit as well!

In the New Testament, John the Baptist prophesied that Jesus would baptize with the Holy Spirit *and* with fire:

> As for me, I baptize you with water for repentance, but He who is coming after me is mightier than I, and I am not fit to remove His sandals; He will baptize you with the Holy Spirit and fire. (Matthew 3:11)

This is what unfolded on the day of Pentecost in Acts 2. Here is how Luke recorded what happened that amazing day:

> When the day of Pentecost had come, they were all together in one place. And suddenly a noise like a violent rushing wind came from heaven, and it filled the whole house where they were sitting. And tongues that looked like fire appeared to them, distributing themselves, and a tongue rested on each one of them.

> And they were all filled with the Holy Spirit and began to speak with different tongues, as the Spirit was giving them the ability to speak out. (Acts 2:1-4)

As John the Baptist had prophesied, Jesus baptized those in attendance that day with the Holy Spirit ("noise like a violent rushing wind") and fire ("tongues… like fire").

Later in the New Testament, the apostle Paul told his protégé, Timothy, about the fire that was burning inside him: the Holy Spirit. He reminded Timothy to fan the flame of the Holy Spirit so that it didn't go out, so that the supernatural fire he was given for preaching and teaching would continue to burn and enable him to make a greater and greater impact for the kingdom. He further reminded Timothy that God had not given him (or us) a spirit of fear or timidity:

> This is why I remind you to fan into flames the spiritual gift God gave you when I laid my hands on you. For God has not given us a spirit of fear and timidity, but of power, love, and self-discipline. (2 Timothy 1:6-7 NLT)

This is *the same power* that Jesus promised the disciples so they could be His witnesses to the world:

> But you will receive power when the Holy Spirit has come upon you; and you shall be My witnesses both in Jerusalem and in all Judea, and Samaria, and as far as the remotest part of the earth. (Acts 1:8)

Notice that Timothy could *not* have received this Holy Spirit power at his salvation. If he had, he would not have needed Paul to lay hands on him and baptize him in the Holy Spirit. Paul said Timothy received this power when he, Paul, laid his hands on him. This is clearly a separate baptism event from Timothy's salvation. It was the moment he was baptized in the Holy Spirit and received power for witnessing, preaching, and teaching, just as the disciples had received at Pentecost.

This is the exact same Holy Spirit power that evangelicals, Baptists, Methodists, and millions of other believers throughout the world today are missing!

Once we receive this Holy Spirit power, we are encouraged to nurture it along with the spiritual gifts we've each been given, as if tending a fire to keep it ever burning and ever useful for the glory of God. This fire is the active presence of the Holy Spirit in those who have received the Spirit baptism, and we need to keep it burning hot, lest it be snuffed out, as Paul encourages us:

Do not quench the Spirit. (1 Thessalonians 5:19)

When we quench the Spirit of God, we extinguish His fire. We snuff it out by failing to follow through on what He's prompting us to do. We are not to extinguish the fire of the Holy Spirit burning inside us. Not even turn it down to a medium or low simmer. It's this roaring fire that is at work in us to refine, purify, and sanctify us away from sin and toward the righteousness and holiness of God. Quenching the Holy Spirit prevents us from growing in Christ, in faith, in righteousness, in holiness, in power, and in effectiveness for the Lord.

Paul wrote in his letter to Titus:

> He saved us, not on the basis of deeds which we did in righteousness, but in accordance with His mercy, **by the washing of regeneration and renewing by the Holy Spirit, whom He richly poured out upon us through Jesus Christ our Savior.** (Titus 3:5-6)

Oil

In scripture, the Holy Spirit is also represented quite often by oil, especially oil for anointings and for producing light.

Anointing Oil

Anointing oil has been used throughout Israel's history to consecrate (set apart) individuals or objects for sacred use. It represented the Spirit's presence and power upon those individuals and objects.

In the Old Testament, for example, priests and temple objects were anointed with oil to consecrate them for service to God:

> Moses then took the anointing oil and anointed the tabernacle and everything that was in it, and consecrated them. He also sprinkled some of it on the altar seven times and anointed the altar and all its utensils, and the basin and its stand, to consecrate them.

> Then he poured some of the anointing oil on Aaron's head and anointed him, to consecrate him. (Leviticus 8:10-12)

As well, the Lord had Samuel anoint David as the next (second) king over Israel:

> So Samuel took the horn of oil and anointed him in the midst of his brothers; and the Spirit of the Lord rushed upon David from that day forward. And Samuel set out and went to Ramah. (1 Samuel 16:13)

The use of anointing oil continued in the New Testament. For example, a few days before Jesus would be crucified, a woman anointed Jesus's head with expensive perfume (scented oil):

> While He was in Bethany at the home of Simon the Leper, He was reclining at the table, and a woman came with an alabaster vial of very expensive perfume of pure nard. She broke the vial and poured the perfume over His head. But there were some indignantly remarking to one another, "Why has this perfume been wasted? For this perfume could have been sold for over three hundred denarii, and the money given to the poor." And they were scolding her. But Jesus said, "Leave her alone! Why are you bothering her? She has done a good deed for Me. For you always have the poor with you, and whenever you want, you can do good to them; but you do not always have Me. She

> has done what she could; she has anointed My body beforehand for the burial. Truly I say to you, wherever the gospel is preached in the entire world, what this woman has done will also be told in memory of her." (Mark 14:3-9)

Jesus was the "Christ," the "Messiah." The Hebrew word for "Messiah" and the Greek word for "Christ" both mean "Anointed One." Christ is not a name but a title—Jesus *the* Christ. And He is just that—the Anointed One. Anointed to be Prophet, Priest, and King.

In Acts 10, God sent Peter (through a vision) to share the Good News of Jesus with a family of Gentiles. Peter's visit represented the first time that salvation would be preached to anyone outside God's chosen nation of Israel. Notice what Peter told this Gentile household:

> And you know that God anointed Jesus of Nazareth with the Holy Spirit and with power. Then Jesus went around doing good and healing all who were oppressed by the devil, for God was with him. (Acts 10:38 NLT)

Jesus was anointed with oil by the woman and with the Holy Spirit and power by His Father (after His water baptism). Jesus *is* the Anointed One. Anointed with oil and the Holy Spirit. Set apart for God's work of salvation for all people.

Oil for Lamps / Lights

In Jesus's parable of the ten virgins (maidens or bridesmaids) in Matthew 25, oil symbolizes the Holy Spirit, not for anointing, but rather for powering a sustaining light.

Ten virgins were going out to meet the bridegroom (Jesus). They would then join the wedding feast. However, they did not know how long the wait would be for the bridegroom to return (Christ's second coming). In the parable, Jesus said that five virgins (representing the believing portion of Israel in the tribulation) were wise but five were foolish (the unbelieving portion of Israel). Not knowing how long the wait would be, the wise virgins kept extra oil with them for their lamps, but the foolish five did not. When the foolish virgins left to buy more oil (because they weren't continually prepared), the bridegroom arrived, and the wise virgins entered the wedding feast. The foolish virgins later returned:

> Yet later, the other virgins also came, saying, "Lord, lord, open up for us." But he answered, "Truly I say to you, I do not know you." Be on the alert then, because you do not know the day nor the hour. (Matthew 25:11-13)

Jesus was warning those who were listening (Jews) that they needed to *always* be prepared for His return, since no one would know the actual day or hour. To be prepared, they would need to remain filled with the Holy Spirit—to keep that fire within them burning bright. Being filled with the world would distract them, causing them to miss the moment of His return. That's exactly what happened to the foolish virgins.

(Note: Jesus's parables, including this one, were part of His earthly ministry to Jews only. They are not for us today, although we should understand them and learn from them. Here, Jesus was talking about His second coming that will occur at the end of the seven-year tribulation period. He told the five foolish virgins that He did not know them because, for them to go and buy oil during the tribulation, they would need to take the mark of the beast, *which would require them to reject Christ* [Revelation 13:16-17]. To buy and sell in that day, they would need to proclaim, "We do not know Him," which is why He told them, "I do not know you.")

We see a foreshadowing of this parable in the book of Exodus. Notice the shift from needing to keep the lamps burning in the presence of the Lord inside the tabernacle to Jesus's parable of each believer in the tribulation keeping their own lamp burning:

> Command the people of Israel to bring you pure oil of pressed olives for the light, to keep the lamps burning continually. The lampstand will stand in the Tabernacle, in front of the inner curtain that shields the Ark of the Covenant. Aaron and his sons must keep the lamps burning in the Lord's presence all night. This is a permanent law for the people of Israel, and it must be observed from generation to generation. (Exodus 27:20-21 NLT)

After God led the Israelites out of Egypt, He established His dwelling place to be in the tabernacle. The tabernacle was the sacred tent that God had the Israelites build and carry with them throughout their forty years in the wilderness. Once they had reached the Promised Land and eventually established a kingdom, King Solomon built the first permanent holy temple in Jerusalem, replacing the tabernacle as God's dwelling place. A second temple was built after the first was destroyed by the Babylonians. King Herod significantly upgraded the second temple during the time of Jesus, but God had the Roman army destroy it in AD 70.

Even though we won't experience the tribulation, you and I are now the temple of God, and the oil that keeps our lamps burning is the Holy Spirit in us:

> Do you not know that you are a temple of God and that the Spirit of God dwells in you? (1 Corinthians 3:16)
>
> Or do you not know that your body is a temple of the Holy Spirit within you, whom you have from God, and that you are not your own? For you have been bought for a price: therefore glorify God in your body. (1 Corinthians 6:19-20)

Water
Water in the Bible often symbolizes the Holy Spirit and His ability to fill us spiritually, refresh us, cleanse us, and be a never-ending flow of spiritual power in us and through us.

Rivers and streams bring never-ending flows of water into and through their environments. They feed, nurture, sustain, and even protect all that rely on them for living an abundant life. This is exactly what the Holy Spirit does for us in our lives.

God reveals to us that water is one way He refreshes and blesses His people:

> For I will pour water on the thirsty land
> And streams on the dry ground;
> I will pour out My Spirit on your offspring,
> And My blessing on your descendants. (Isaiah 44:3)

To the woman at the well, Jesus said:

> Everyone who drinks of this water will be thirsty again; but whoever drinks of the water that I will give him shall never be thirsty; but the water that I will give him will become in him a fountain of water springing up to eternal life. (John 4:13-14)

Jesus went on to preach this living water to the Jews gathered at the Feast of Tabernacles:

> Now on the last day, the great day of the feast, Jesus stood and cried out, saying, "If anyone is thirsty, let him come to Me and drink. The one who believes in Me, as the Scripture said, 'From his innermost being will flow rivers of living water.'" But this He said in reference to the Spirit, whom those who believed in Him were to receive; for the Spirit was not yet given, because Jesus was not yet glorified. (John 7:37-39)

The Holy Spirit *is* this "living water." And He will flow endlessly from within us and out to the world as a blessing from God.

Have you ever left a faucet or garden hose running? To us, it's a waste of water, but the opposite is true of the Holy Spirit. He can and should be flowing through us non-stop, without any interruption. When we quench Him, it's like pinching the hose and cutting Him off. Or we could say He's like electricity flowing through power lines to light up a city. The power can certainly be shut off, but why do that when the result is so beautiful, bright, and beneficial?

So, go ahead, turn on the faucet or flip the light switch of the Holy Spirit. But don't quench Him. Don't cut Him off. Don't prevent Him from working. Let His power, the very power of God, continually work in you and through you to the glory of God!

Holy Spirit Highlights—Old Testament

The presence and role of the Holy Spirit was different in the Old Testament than in the New Testament. He was still active but more hidden prior to Christ's coming. Let's explore some of His appearances from "In the beginning" until Matthew's gospel.

As we saw earlier, the Holy Spirit existed from before the world began and was even present at creation:

> In the beginning God created the heavens and the earth. And the earth was a formless and desolate emptiness, and darkness was over the surface of the deep, and the Spirit of God was hovering over the surface of the waters. (Genesis 1:1-2)

He interpreted dreams on behalf of God, as He did for Joseph:

> Then Pharaoh said to his servants, "Can we find a man like this, in whom there is a divine spirit?" So Pharaoh said to Joseph, "Since God has informed you of all this, there is no one as discerning and wise as you are." (Genesis 41:38-39)

He filled men with wisdom, understanding, knowledge, creativity, and craftsmanship:

> Now the Lord spoke to Moses, saying, "See, I have called by name Bezalel, the son of Uri, the son of Hur, of the tribe of Judah. And I have filled him with the Spirit of God in wisdom, in understanding, in knowledge, and in all kinds of craftsmanship, to create artistic designs for work in gold, in silver, and in bronze, and in the cutting of stones for settings, and in the carving of wood, so that he may work in all kinds of craftsmanship." (Exodus 31:1-5)

The Holy Spirit came upon men to cover them for leadership and service:

> So the Spirit of the Lord covered Gideon like clothing; and he blew a trumpet, and the Abiezrites were called together to follow him. (Judges 6:34)

He gave men physical strength:

> Then Samson went down to Timnah with his father and mother, and came as far as the vineyards of Timnah; and behold, a young lion came roaring toward him. And the Spirit of the Lord rushed upon him, so that he tore it apart as one tears apart a young goat, though he had nothing in his hand; but he did not tell his father or mother what he had done. (Judges 14:5-6)

He entered men that God called to be prophets:

> Then He said to me, "Son of man, stand on your feet, and I will speak with you." And as He spoke to me the Spirit entered me and set me on my feet; and I heard Him speaking to me. Then He said to me, "Son of man, I am sending you to the sons of Israel, to a rebellious people who have rebelled against Me; they and their fathers have revolted against Me to this very day." (Ezekiel 2:1-3)

And spoke through female prophets as well (including Miriam, Deborah, and Anna):

> Above all, you must realize that no prophecy in Scripture ever came from the prophet's own understanding, or from human initiative. No, those prophets were moved by the Holy Spirit, and they spoke from God. (2 Peter 1:20-21 NLT)

Holy Spirit Highlights—New Testament

And here are a few instances where the Holy Spirit shows up in the New Testament, revealing His power, abilities, and work among believers.

He testifies:

> The Spirit Himself testifies with our spirit that we are children of God. (Romans 8:16)

He guides us away from sin:

> But I say, walk by the Spirit, and you will not carry out the desire of the flesh. (Galatians 5:16)

He conceived Jesus:

> Now the birth of Jesus the Messiah was as follows: when His mother Mary had been betrothed to Joseph, before they came together she was found to be pregnant by the Holy Spirit. (Matthew 1:18)

He led Jesus in the wilderness:

> Now Jesus, full of the Holy Spirit, returned from the Jordan and was led around by the Spirit in the wilderness. (Luke 4:1)

He empowered Jesus:

> And Jesus returned to Galilee in the power of the Spirit, and news about Him spread through all the surrounding region. (Luke 4:14)

He further empowered Jesus in fulfillment of Isaiah's prophecy (Isaiah 61):

> And He came to Nazareth, where He had been brought up; and as was His custom, He entered the synagogue on the Sabbath, and stood up to read. And the scroll of Isaiah the prophet was handed to Him. And He unrolled the scroll and found the place where it was written:
>
> "The Spirit of the Lord is upon Me,
> Because He anointed Me to bring good news to the poor.
> He has sent Me to proclaim release to captives,
> And recovery of sight to the blind,
> To set free those who are oppressed,
> To proclaim the favorable year of the Lord." (Luke 4:16-19)

He teaches us:

> These things I have spoken to you while remaining with you. But the Helper, the Holy Spirit whom the Father will send in My name, He will teach you all things, and remind you of all that I said to you. (John 14:25-26)

He convicts us:

> And He, when He comes, will convict the world regarding sin, and righteousness, and judgment: regarding sin, because they do not believe in Me; and regarding righteousness, because I am going to the Father and you no longer are going to see Me; and regarding judgment, because the ruler of this world has been judged. (John 16:8-11)

He guides us into truth:

> I have many more things to say to you, but you cannot bear them at the present time. But when He, the Spirit of truth, comes, He will guide you into all the truth; for He will not speak on His own, but whatever He hears, He will speak; and He will disclose to you what is to come. (John 16:12-13)

He glorifies Jesus:

> He will glorify Me, for He will take from Mine and will disclose it to you. (John 16:14)

He seals us for eternity:

> In Him, you also, after listening to the message of truth, the gospel of your salvation—having also believed, you were sealed in Him with the Holy Spirit of the promise. (Ephesians 1:13)

He fills us with His "fruit of the Spirit":

> But the fruit of the Spirit is love, joy, peace, patience, kindness, goodness, faithfulness, gentleness, self-control; against such things there is no law. (Galatians 5:22-23)

He works His supernatural gifts through those who have been Spirit-baptized:

> For to one is given the word of wisdom through the Spirit, and to another the word of knowledge according to the same Spirit; to another faith by the same Spirit, and to another gifts of healing by the one Spirit, and to another the effecting of miracles, and to another prophecy, and to another the distinguishing of spirits, to another various kinds of tongues, and to another the interpretation of tongues. But one and the same Spirit works all these things, distributing to each one individually just as He wills. (1 Corinthians 12:8-11)

He physically moves people:

> When they came up out of the water, the Spirit of the Lord snatched Philip away; and the eunuch no longer saw him, but went on his way rejoicing. (Acts 8:39)

He gives life to those who are saved:

> He has enabled us to be ministers of his new covenant. This is a covenant not of written laws, but of the Spirit. The old written covenant ends in death; but under the new covenant, the Spirit gives life. (2 Corinthians 3:6 NLT)

He guides believers away from trouble and toward righteousness/righteous work:

> Next Paul and Silas traveled through the area of Phrygia and Galatia, because the Holy Spirit had prevented them from preaching the word in the province of Asia at that time. Then coming to the borders of Mysia, they headed north for the province of Bithynia, but again the Spirit of Jesus did not allow them to go there. So instead, they went on through Mysia to the seaport of Troas. That night Paul had a vision: A man from Macedonia in northern Greece was standing there, pleading with him, "Come over to Macedonia and help us!" So we decided to leave for Macedonia at once, having concluded that God was calling us to preach the Good News there. (Acts 16:6-10 NLT)

He helps believers pray:

> And the Holy Spirit helps us in our weakness. For example, we don't know what God wants us to pray for. But the Holy Spirit prays for us with groanings that cannot be expressed in words. And the Father who knows all hearts knows what the Spirit is saying, for the Spirit pleads for us believers in harmony with God's own will. (Romans 8:26-27 NLT)

We can build up our faith by praying in the Holy Spirit:

> But you, beloved, building yourselves up on your most holy faith, praying in the Holy Spirit... (Jude 1:20)

He demonstrates God's power through believers:

> And my message and my preaching were not in persuasive words of wisdom, but in demonstration of the Spirit and of power, so that your faith would not rest on the wisdom of mankind, but on the power of God. (1 Corinthians 2:4-5)

He strengthens us with power on the inside:

> ... that He would grant you, according to the riches of His glory, to be strengthened with power through His Spirit in the inner self... (Ephesians 3:16)

Fruit of the Spirit

In Galatians 5, Paul tells us that there are two spirits at work in every believer. There is the spirit of the flesh: a condition that all are born with thanks to our ancestor, Adam, and his free-will choice to sin against God. Believers, though, also have the Spirit of God at work in them. This dramatically differentiates us from the world, from those who live with only the spirit of the flesh and without the Spirit of God.

These two spirits battle constantly within us, a reality every believer knows all too well. But in Galatians 5:16, we are called to "walk by the Spirit" so that we don't "carry out the desire of the flesh." Paul then writes that others can see who we're allowing to win this battle within us—by the fruit we bear in our lives:

> Now the deeds of the flesh are evident, which are: sexual immorality, impurity, indecent behavior, idolatry, witchcraft, hostilities, strife, jealousy, outbursts of anger, selfish ambition, dissensions, factions, envy, drunkenness, carousing, and things like these, of which I forewarn you, just as I have forewarned you, that those who practice such things will not inherit the kingdom of God. But the fruit of the Spirit is love, joy, peace, patience, kindness, goodness, faithfulness, gentleness, self-control; against such things there is no law. (Galatians 5:19-23)

We receive the Holy Spirit and His "fruit" in the moment of our conversion. This fruit should flow from us naturally and without effort because of our new heart and mind in Christ Jesus. We do, though, need to give the Holy Spirit time to sanctify us, to make us more and more righteous and holy, but that fight is very real. Over time, our fruit must move from being produced out of selfish, fleshly desires to being solely the bountiful fruit of the Holy Spirit.

We can work *with* the Holy Spirit to produce kingdom fruit by fully surrendering our life and will to God, by being obedient to Him and His Word, by forgiving others (letting go of bitterness), by not quenching the Spirit, and by not grieving the Spirit:

> Do not quench the Spirit. (1 Thessalonians 5:19)

> Do not grieve the Holy Spirit of God, by whom you were sealed for the day of redemption. (Ephesians 4:30)

Supernatural Gifts of the Holy Spirit

Paul writes in 1 Corinthians 12 that the Holy Spirit manifests His supernatural gifts *anytime* and *at His will*. Humans cannot make these gifts operate by our own effort or will. Nor can we call up the Holy Spirit to work His power as if He's a genie in a bottle. No matter how much we desire to or how much we feel as though we can, scripture does not support these ideas in any way. After all, the point of the Holy Spirit and His spiritual gifts is to work *His* power through us, which *we do not possess*.

We won't look at these nine gifts in any detail in this book, but here is the list as recorded in 1 Corinthians 12:4-11:

1. word of wisdom
2. word of knowledge

3. faith
4. gifts of healings
5. the effecting of miracles
6. prophecy
7. distinguishing of spirits
8. various kinds of tongues
9. the interpretation of tongues

It is important to understand that the Holy Spirit only works His supernatural gifts through believers who are Spirit-baptized. And these gifts are still for today!

Nothing in scripture—*nothing*—states or indicates that these gifts have ceased. God is still on the throne. Jesus is still seated at His right hand. And the Holy Spirit and His supernatural gifts are still at work in the lives of believers today. What *has* ceased, though, unfortunately, is belief in the Holy Spirit, belief in His power, and belief in His supernatural gifts. This harms and weakens individual believers as well as the entire Body of Christ and its kingdom work.

As we've just seen, the Holy Spirit is our helper and guide and power. He has been at work in believers and in the world since before "In the beginning." But for the last two thousand years, during this age of grace (which began with Christ's crucifixion), He has dwelled both within *and* upon believers.

He indwells us to continually sanctify us, to convict us away from sin and toward righteousness. He also comes upon us with power through the baptism in the Holy Spirit—power for growing the Body of Christ through witnessing and power for building up the Body of Christ.

So, while God the Father oversees and directs all things, God the Son *is* all things (the Way, the Truth, the Life, the

Word, Light, Savior, High Priest, King, Kinsman Redeemer, etc.). The Holy Spirit, then, is actively fulfilling His own work on earth and in believers, bringing about God's will, especially His plan of redemption and salvation for all people.

4

The Truth About the Book of Acts

Why the Book of Acts?
THE BOOK OF Acts is not a fairy-tale full of cotton candy rainbows and English garden tea parties. This is what I had been led to believe, though. Then I studied the book for myself. It's more like a supernatural espionage thriller full of intrigue, betrayal, twists, turns, and a little bit of blood. But, in the end, God wins, and the church survives.

Why, then, is Acts so important to include in a book about salvations and baptisms? Because Acts is filled with them—salvations and baptisms—most of which seem odd or out of place or even contradictory. This chapter will bring clarity to our topic by answering questions and clearing up confusion about this amazing book.

The confusion certainly isn't intentional on God's part or even Luke's, the writer of Acts. It simply results from the book being transitional *and* historical. Too many denominations, pastors, and teachers, though, use it for doctrine, which is a huge mistake, or they pull bits and pieces out of context or ignore the book completely.

Doctrine simply means "teaching." For those of the Christian faith, then, doctrine is teaching to be followed, put into practice at church and in life so we can live out our faith the way God intended.

But biblical doctrine can't be inconsistent or contradictory. That's exactly where the Body of Christ is today, though:

> As a result, we are no longer to be children, tossed here and there by waves and carried about by every wind of doctrine, by the trickery of people, by craftiness in deceitful scheming; (Ephesians 4:14)

Just because a verse exists in the Bible doesn't mean it can be used for doctrine. If it's in the Bible, then it certainly is God's truth. But not all truth—not all of God's Word—is meant as doctrine for us today.

It's important for us to understand the context of all scripture—who was writing, to whom, when, where, and for what purpose. If we pull scripture out of context or twist its meaning to fit our wishes, we will confuse people and create serious conflict between denominations, churches, and individual believers in the Body of Christ. God did not intend for His Word to divide us; He intended it to bring unity.

Pulling doctrine out of the Old Testament or from Jesus's earthly ministry, which was specific to Jews, drives disunity in the Body.

Christian doctrine for today should come only from Paul's writings. Afterall, Jesus had called him to be the apostle to the Gentiles, our apostle for today:

But the Lord said to him [Ananias], "Go, for he [Saul/Paul] is a chosen instrument of Mine, to bear My Name before the Gentiles and kings and the sons of Israel; (Acts 9:15)

Instead, they saw that God had given me the responsibility of preaching the gospel to the Gentiles, just as he [God] had given Peter the responsibility of preaching to the Jews. For the same God who worked through Peter as the apostle to the Jews also worked through me as the apostle to the Gentiles.

In fact, James, Peter, and John, who were known as pillars of the church, recognized the gift God had given me, and they accepted Barnabas and me as their co-workers. They encouraged us to keep preaching to the Gentiles, while they continued their work with the Jews. (Galatians 2:7-9 NLT)

God also revealed several mysteries to Paul that He had not revealed to *anyone* before in history, even to Old Testament prophets. Aside from one, these mysteries were specific for the grace age and not for the nation of Israel, including:

- The mystery of the gospel of grace (Romans 16:25-26)
- The mystery of the rapture (1 Corinthians 15:51-53; 1 Thessalonians 4:13-18)
- The mystery of the church/Body of Christ (Ephesians 3:1-10)

- The mystery of godliness (1 Timothy 3:16)
- The mystery of Christ in us (Colossians 1:25-27)
- The mystery of the hardening of Israel (Romans 11:25-26)

And Paul's letters were certainly biblical truth:

The sum of Your word is truth,
And every one of Your righteous judgments is everlasting. (Psalm 119:160)

Sanctify them in the truth; Your word is truth. (John 17:17)

There are churches and denominations today that say scripture *requires* water baptism for salvation. Not water-baptized? To hell with you—literally!

There are others who claim scripture says *not* to water-baptize at all. If you do, they maintain, you're adding works to your salvation when we are saved by faith alone.

And still others say it is optional for every believer. So, hey, let's just flip a coin.

One of the biggest mistakes many make is to take one situation of salvation or baptism from the book of Acts and claim that it is doctrine for all Christians for all time. For example, to take what happened with the Holy Spirit coming upon Cornelius's household in Acts 10—empowering them to speak in tongues—does not create a doctrine for the church so that when the Holy Spirit falls upon believers, they *must* immediately speak in tongues or it's evidence that they're not filled with the Holy Ghost. This is not biblical and can easily be disproven.

Just because something is in the Bible, or even in the New Testament, does *not* mean it is *our pattern for today.*

There are denominations that pull "tongues" doctrine from this passage and refer to it as initial evidence of Spirit baptism. But these denominations apply just that one part of this passage. These new believers in Cornelius's house didn't say a prayer nor did anyone pray over them. No one laid hands on them either. And they were baptized in water *after* the Holy Spirit fell on them. Why not follow these aspects of the verses as well? Why neglect to include them in a tongues doctrine?

There are multiple other salvations and Spirit baptisms in Acts that contradict what happened in Chapter 10. For example, in Acts 16, Paul led a Gentile jailer and his household to salvation. But the Holy Spirit did not fall on them and they failed to speak in tongues.

Acts cannot be used to determine doctrine. If it were, then every church and denomination could pick and choose which events from the book they would use for doctrine and which they would ignore. There is no pattern or consistency in the book of Acts that leads the Body of Christ to stay in unity with doctrine. But we now find ourselves in serious disunity. We hold family food fights in public, pounding the table in disagreement and demeaning each other with cameras rolling while unbelievers look elsewhere for truth.

Seems quite messy and unbiblical to me.

The book of Acts is *transitional and historical only.*

The church today—the Body of Christ—must pull its teachings and doctrines solely from the letters of the apostle

Paul (Romans through Philemon). Jesus called Paul specifically to be our apostle for today, in this age of grace.

Paul stated the tongues issue quite simply:

> I wish you could all speak in tongues, but even more I wish you could all prophesy. For prophecy is greater than speaking in tongues, unless someone interprets what you are saying so that the whole church will be strengthened. (1 Corinthians 14:5 NLT)

That settles it! Paul was clear that not all believers speak in tongues. In fact, he stated he'd rather believers prophesy than speak in tongues because tongues edify the individual while prophecy edifies the whole Body (1 Corinthians 14:4).

Doctrinal errors are especially harmful to the Body of Christ when it comes to witnessing, salvation, water baptisms, spirit baptisms, and speaking in tongues.

The book of Acts is not prescriptive; it is only descriptive. It describes *what did happen*; it does not prescribe what *should happen*. While it is of course scripture, it is not for doctrine, but simply records thirty to forty years of first-century Jewish and church history.

Overview of Acts

Regarding Luke, the writer, he was not a disciple of Jesus nor an apostle. He was a Gentile physician who became a traveling companion of the apostle Paul during one of Paul's missionary journeys. Not much else is known about him except that he was quite skilled at documenting detailed accounts of events he witnessed himself or that he'd heard directly from eyewitnesses.

Chapter 1 of Acts begins with Christ's ascension to heaven, followed by the selection of Matthias to replace Judas Iscariot as the twelfth disciple (or apostle). Acts ends in Chapter 28 with Paul imprisoned in Rome even as he continued to preach and write. In between, you will find the type of action, adventure, and drama more common to the Old Testament and Clint Eastwood Westerns.

The full title of the book is "Acts of the Apostles." But Paul is by far mentioned more than the other apostles, who'd all spent three years with Jesus. There is no evidence that Paul ever met Jesus. As a Pharisee, though, he worked hard to imprison and kill Jews who chose to follow Christ.

Peter is a distant second in number of times appearing in the book of Acts. After Chapter 10, it's mostly Acts of the Apostle Paul, with no mention of Peter after Chapter 15.

Other appropriate titles might be: Acts of the Holy Spirit (who is more active here than in the Old Testament), History of the Early Church, or The Fall of Israel.

That last one is my favorite. I heard it first from the late Les Feldick, the renowned Oklahoma rancher/farmer and prolific Bible teacher.

Acts does in fact lightly record the fall of Israel in the first century, which was directly related to the establishment and subsequent growth of the early Christian church. It is no coincidence that as Israel fell, Christianity rose. Paul wrote this in Romans:

> I say then, they [Israel] did not stumble so as to fall, did they? Far from it! But by their wrongdoing salvation has come to the Gentiles, to make them [Israel] jealous. Now if their wrongdoing proves to be riches

for the world, and their failure, riches for the Gentiles, how much more will their fulfillment be! (Romans 11:11-12)

As a result of Israel rejecting Jesus as their prophesied Messiah (by crucifying Him), God used the Roman army to destroy the Jewish temple in AD 70, which Jesus had prophesied in Mark 13:1-4. The Romans then went on to destroy the city of Jerusalem, driving all Jews out of the city and eventually out of Judea, dispersing them to other nations near and far. They would not return to their homeland and become a nation again until 1948—nearly two thousand years later! Keep reading your Bible and watching the news and you will see that God is not done with Israel, His chosen people.

The book of Acts is packed with salvations and baptisms and stories of faith, but also layered with adventure and drama. Inside its twenty-eight chapters, you'll read about murder, attempted murder, trials, stonings, teleportation, jailbreaks, people dropping dead for lying, shipwrecks, snake bites, exorcisms, and even business disruptions.

For our purposes, though, here are the three areas of Acts we'll focus on in this chapter:

- History and Transition: New Wine, Old Wineskins
- What Really Happened at Pentecost?
- A Brief Outline of the Book of Acts

History and Transition: New Wine, Old Wineskins

As mentioned in the previous section, the book of Acts is historical and transitional, not doctrinal. We cannot draw out of the book any church standards or doctrines. There's just too much inconsistency because of the overlap or "collision" of Old Testament covenant law with its focus on Israel versus God's new program of grace and focus on Gentiles and the church (Body of Christ).

Acts simply records the "acts" of the apostles as they experienced the monumental transition from the *pre-crucifixion* age of the law and prophets to the *post-crucifixion* age of grace and the church.

(Note: The Jewish Torah, or Pentateuch, comprises the first five books of the Old Testament—Genesis, Exodus, Leviticus, Numbers, and Deuteronomy. For Israel, these were and are the books of the law. When Moses descended Mount Sinai, he didn't just bring down two stone tablets containing the Ten Commandments; God had also given him the law and writings for the Torah.)

The transition recorded in the book of Acts was pretty, well, ugly. It was not a happy-go-lucky time. The changeover from law to grace wasn't clean, clear, or concise. Transitions in life rarely are because humans are involved. Think selfishness, pride, power, and greed. Luke recorded a lot of arguments and in-fighting that occurred throughout these years, quite a bit of it from among the apostles and fellow Jewish believers, but also with religious, nonbelieving Jews as well.

This distressing transition, though, was unavoidable. Jesus, a Jew who followed the law from birth throughout His death, could not carry out His ministry, fulfill His work on the cross, and then resurrect without difficulties. That would have required the Jewish-believing culture and the new Gentile-believing culture to immediately hold hands and sing "Kumbaya" in unison. Such a sudden shift would have been impossible given God's fresh new program of grace *fully* apart from the law. It proved to be a bloody, impossible shift, especially for the Jewish people, but it was a shift that Jesus had prophesied:

> And no one pours new wine into old wineskins; otherwise the new wine will burst the skins and it will be spilled out, and the skins will be ruined. But new wine must be put into fresh wineskins. And no one, after drinking old wine wants new; for he says, "The old is fine." (Luke 5:37-39)

Jesus said this in response to some Pharisees complaining that He was hanging out with tax collectors and sinners (including his newly chosen disciple, Matthew). These sinners were open to new teachings, a new way of salvation that didn't involve laws impossible to follow and enforced by hypocritical religious leaders. The old just didn't satisfy these sinners in search of salvation. In fact, it turned them off.

For Israelites to fully drink in this new covenant—sealed with the blood of Christ—they would first need to shed the old covenant with its hardened laws and traditions. Religious Jews, those who thought they were righteous by their own works, were not open to this new message. That's why Jesus said for them, "The old wine is fine." In fact, they hated the new wine so much, they killed the Vintner's Son.

Those who knew they were sinners, though, loved Jesus from their first taste of Him, and they certainly felt His love for them.

We Gentiles today are not tethered to that old covenant, to Jewish laws or their traditions. We taste Christ and immediately thirst for more.

I do believe that a rapid shift from old to new was God's intent, but Jewish religious leaders (including those who became believers in Christ) were not going to allow their fifteen hundred years of Mosaic law and traditions (and their control of it) be so easily tossed aside. That would have killed their entrenched power and influence. This was just part of what Jesus meant by His final words on the cross: "It is finished" (John 19:30).

"It is finished" was a message from Jesus to every Jew about what they had just witnessed. Most rejected it (by rejecting Him), while the rest simply didn't understand what was happening.

Through Christ's death on the cross, the Old Testament law and prophets were fulfilled, ushering in God's new age of grace and the church. Here is just a small sampling of what Jesus meant by, "It is finished."

He was the final Passover lamb—temple sacrifices were no longer necessary:

> First, Christ said, "You did not want animal sacrifices or sin offerings or burnt offerings or other offerings for sin, nor were you pleased with them" (though they are required by the law of Moses). Then he said, "Look, I have come to do your will." He cancels the

first covenant in order to put the second into effect. For God's will was for us to be made holy by the sacrifice of the body of Jesus Christ, once for all time. (Hebrews 10:8-10 NLT)

He fulfilled the law and the prophets—He satisfied them:

Don't misunderstand why I have come. I did not come to abolish the law of Moses or the writings of the prophets. No, I came to accomplish their purpose. (Matthew 5:17 NLT)

The temple veil was torn, giving all believers direct access to the Father:

Then Jesus shouted out again, and he released his spirit. At that moment the curtain in the sanctuary of the Temple was torn in two, from top to bottom. The earth shook, rocks split apart. (Matthew 27:50-51 NLT)

He conquered sin because we could not:

For the sin of this one man, Adam, caused death to rule over many. But even greater is God's wonderful grace and his gift of righteousness, for all who receive it will live in triumph over sin and death through this one man, Jesus Christ. (Romans 5:17 NLT)

He conquered death so that we might have life—abundant and everlasting life:

> For God so loved the world, that He gave His only Son, so that everyone who believes in Him will not perish, but have eternal life. (John 3:16)

> The thief comes only to steal and kill and destroy; I came so that they would have life, and have it abundantly. (John 10:10)

Paul further explained the beautiful reason that believers then and now need to let go of the law and look solely to Jesus as the *only way* of being forgiven, justified, and forever in right standing with God the Father:

> So now there is no condemnation for those who belong to Christ Jesus. And because you belong to him, the power of the life-giving Spirit has freed you from the power of sin that leads to death. The law of Moses was unable to save us because of the weakness of our sinful nature. So God did what the law could not do. He sent his own Son in a body like the bodies we sinners have. And in that body God declared an end to sin's control over us by giving his Son as a sacrifice for our sins. (Romans 8:1-3 NLT)

Through His Son's crucifixion, the book of Acts reveals how God shifted His program of salvation away from the age of law and blood sacrifices to the age of grace. Instead of a quick flip of the switch, though, a gradual, and painful, transition unfolded. Those thirty to forty years of transition were harsh in terms of how Israel fell and how the church took root, slowly formed, and grew.

To bring some clarity to the confusion, here are the basic groups of people that existed during the period of Acts:

- Jews—who fully rejected Christ and continued to follow the law

- Jews—who were baptized into John the Baptist's baptism but continued to follow the law (which Paul warned them against doing)

- Jews—who were baptized in the name of Jesus but were also forcing Gentiles to convert to Judaism first, get circumcised, follow the law, and only then become a Christian

- Jews—who were saved by the blood of Jesus Christ and left the law and prophets behind, as God intended

- Proselytes—Gentiles who had converted to Judaism

- Gentiles—anyone not a Jew; pagan worshippers who remained in pagan worship and wanted nothing to do with God

- Gentile believers—who were saved by the grace of God and blood of Christ

There certainly were other religious groups in the mix, especially multiple Jewish sects, but they would fall under the first category—Jews who fully rejected Christ. The groups listed above were all in the fight—either fighting for the survival of the Christian church or fighting for its destruction.

As these disparate groups each battled for their own "truth," the overlap of and interactions among Judaism and Christianity grew more complex, and the transition from the law and the prophets to grace and the church intensified. This resulted in more confusion and conflict, but also crippling disagreements and death.

Doctrinal Danger

If we were to try and pull salvation or baptism doctrine out of the book of Acts, we would end up with a confused mess of denominations (or a mess of confused denominations) that fiercely disagree with one another on those beliefs and doctrines. Oh, wait…

Here is just one example of the mess that unfolded during this transition period:

> Some men [Jews] came down from Judea and began teaching the brothers [new Gentile believers], "Unless you are circumcised according to the custom of Moses, you cannot be saved." And after Paul and Barnabas had a heated argument and debate with them, the brothers determined that Paul and Barnabas and some others of them should go up to Jerusalem to the apostles and elders concerning this issue. (Acts 15:1-2)

The remainder of Acts 15 records a crucial event in the history of the Christian church: the Council at Jerusalem. James (the half-brother of Jesus) led the apostles in settling this severe disagreement about demanding Gentile men be circumcised *before* they could be "saved." The ultimate decision to not require the circumcision of Gentile believers truly rescued the church from certain demise before it had barely gotten started.

This courageous decision to spare Gentiles from forever being shackled to Judaic law allowed the Christian church to take hold and flourish. This is just one more reason to appreciate the apostle Paul and the burden he carried to battle for and save what Christ began on the cross.

God never intended for Gentile believers to follow the law. Paul even pressed Jews to let go of the law themselves and receive Jesus as their Messiah, discarding the legal shackles they'd dragged around for fifteen hundred years.

Once Christ was crucified, buried, and resurrected, salvation became available *solely* by God's grace + our faith + nothing else. No words. No works. No circumcision. No animal sacrifices. No water baptism. No striving to keep the Ten Commandments. And, certainly, no reliance on another human being to sit in God's place and forgive our sins.

We have *already* been forgiven. We don't need a second opinion… by anyone. It is finished.

Jesus paid the full and painful price for your sins and mine. He did it two thousand years ago. It is done. There is *nothing* we can do to improve on what He already accomplished for us. We can't improve on His blood, His death, His burial, or His resurrection. Nothing. We simply need to *believe* in what He accomplished on the cross. Not one thing more.

And lest anyone thinks believing or faith itself is a work, Paul set us straight:

> But people are counted as righteous, not because of their work, but because of their faith in God who forgives sinners. (Romans 4:5 NLT)

In those thirty to forty years after His crucifixion, Christ's work on the cross to cover the sins of the whole world was not fully understood. The book of Acts reveals the messiness at play, recording the differing approaches to salvation and baptism.

Table 1 lists all salvation events recorded in the book of Acts, along with any related water and Spirit baptisms—eleven events in all. Notice that no patterns emerge. This is due to the transitional nature of the book as it records God shifting His program of forgiveness for sins from Old Testament animal sacrifices, then to Jesus and John the Baptist preaching repentance and water baptism to Jews, and finally to God subtly introducing His new program of salvation through the blood of His Son.

"Subtly" is accurate. While Jesus's death, burial, and resurrection were anything but subtle, no one, especially His disciples, understood the significance of His blood sacrifice. They were only preaching and pointing to *who Jesus was*—the Son of God—and that He was resurrected. *No one*, including the disciples, had yet begun preaching salvation by the grace of God or by the blood of Christ.

With the destruction of the temple in AD 70, which abruptly ended ritual animal sacrifices, God's only remaining means for forgiveness of sins for all people—including Jews—was (and still is) through the blood of His Son. This is the Good News! This is the gospel that saves today:

> Let me now remind you, dear brothers and sisters of the Good News I preached to you before. You welcomed it then, and you still stand firm in it. It is this Good News that saves you if you continue to believe the message I told you—unless, of course, you believed something that was never true in the first place. I passed on to you what was most important and what had also been passed on to me. Christ died for our sins, just as the Scriptures said. He was buried, and he was raised from the dead on the third day, just as the Scriptures said. (1 Corinthians 15:1-4 NLT)

As shown in Table 1, none of the salvation events in the book of Acts were based on grace nor the blood of Christ covering sins. Peter was close when he preached to Cornelius and his household, but he didn't mention Christ's blood as a covering for their sin. He focused more on the fact that He rose from the dead:

> We are witnesses of all the things that He did both in the country of the Jews and in Jerusalem. They also put Him to death by hanging Him on a cross. God raised Him up on the third day and granted that He be revealed, not to all the people, but to witnesses who had been chosen beforehand by God, that is, to us who ate and drank with Him after He arose from the dead. (Acts 10:39-41)

Book of Acts—Conversions & Baptisms

Who	Jew/Gentile	1st Experience	2nd	3rd	Location
Jesus's disciples	Jew	**Water baptism** for repentance by John or a disciple of Jesus	**Salvation** John 20:22	**Spirit baptism** Acts 2 by God/Jesus	Jerusalem
Pentecost attendees (3,000!)	Jew	**Salvation** Acts 2:37-38 + indwelling of Holy Spirit	**Water baptism** Acts 2:41 by the apostles	**Spirit baptism** No evidence if or when	Jerusalem
Those at Peter's second sermon (5,000!)	Jew	**Salvation** Acts 4:4	**Water baptism** Not recorded	**Spirit baptism** No evidence if or when	Jerusalem
Samaritans	Part Jew / Part Pagan	**Salvation** Acts 8:12-13 + indwelling of Holy Spirit	**Water baptism** Acts 8:12-13 by Philip	**Spirit baptism** Acts 8:14-17 Peter & John pray for them	Samaria
Ethiopian eunuch	God-fearing, but not full proselyte to Judaism	**Salvation** Acts 8:34-36 + indwelling of Holy Spirit	**Water baptism** Acts 8:38 by Philip	**Spirit baptism** No evidence if or when	Road to Gaza

— Table 1 —

Who	Jew/Gentile	1st Experience	2nd	3rd	Location
Saul of Tarsus (Paul)	Jew	**Salvation** Acts 9:3-6 + indwelling of Holy Spirit Acts 9:17-18	**Water baptism** Acts 9:17-18 by Ananias	**Spirit baptism** Acts 9:17-18 by God/Jesus	Road to Damascus
Cornelius & his household	Gentile	**Salvation** Acts 10:34-43	**Spirit baptism** Acts 10:44 by God/Jesus	**Water baptism** Acts 10:48 by Peter	Caesarea
Lydia	Likely a God-fearing Gentile (proselyte to Judaism)	**Salvation** Acts 16:14	**Water baptism** Acts 16:15 by Paul	**Spirit baptism** No evidence if or when	Philippi (Greece)
Jailer & his household	Gentile	**Salvation** Acts 16:29-32	**Water baptism** Acts 16:33 by Paul	**Spirit baptism** No evidence if or when	Philippi
Crispus, his household	Jew	**Salvation** Acts 18:8	**Water baptism** Acts 18:8 by Paul	**Spirit baptism** No evidence if or when	Corinth (Greece)
Disciples at Ephesus	Jew	**Water baptism** first by John the Baptist, then by Paul Acts 19:5	**Salvation** Acts 19:5	**Spirit baptism** Acts 19:6 Paul laid hands on them	Ephesus (Greece)

— Table 1 — (cont.)

This might seem nitpicky, but it's not. If we want to see people saved today, we must be able to tell them exactly what the Bible teaches about *how* to be saved. And that *how* is the Good News that Paul wrote in 1 Corinthians 15:1-4, which Jesus revealed directly to him.

Peter (and his fellow apostles) emphasized the resurrection and witnesses to the resurrection because they were a visual sign of the Messiah. Jews need signs to believe. Gentiles don't. We believe by faith. In a sense, Jews were "trained" to seek out signs from God so they could believe. This began back in Exodus when Moses threw his staff on the ground so God could turn it into a snake. This sign (miracle) was to prove the power of God to Pharoah, but it was a sign to Moses and Aaron as well. A sign that proved God was who He said He was, that He was with them, and that He had the power and faithfulness to fulfill His promises.

Of course, God performed many more miracles for the Israelites in Egypt, then throughout their forty-year journey in the wilderness and their military conquests as they entered Canaan, followed by centuries of signs and miracles that continue even to this day. Since the time of Moses, Jews seek for a sign to always know that God is still with them and still faithful:

> For indeed Jews ask for signs and Greeks search for wisdom. (1 Corinthians 1:22)

Consider what Thomas, one of the twelve disciples, said after hearing of Christ's resurrection:

> So the other disciples were saying to him, "We have seen the Lord!" But he said to them, "Unless I see in His hands the imprint of the nails, and put my finger into the place of the nails, and put my hand into His side, I will not believe." (John 20:25)

We now refer to this disciple as Doubting Thomas. Paul clarifies, though, that Gentile believers don't need signs to believe:

> For we walk by faith, not by sight. (2 Corinthians 5:7)

Peter did not understand why God sent him to Cornelius's home or even what to do once he'd arrived. It was "illegal" for him to even be in the home of a Gentile or to associate with one in any way. But God had called him there, so he simply shared the story of Jesus, then the Holy Spirit did the "heart" work of salvation.

Today, we Gentiles are saved by faith and walk by faith alone, not by sight. We also do not need to follow *any* Old Testament laws, for Christ is our completion of the law:

> For Christ is the end of the Law for righteousness to everyone who believes. (Romans 10:4)

Does this mean that Christians can go out and break these laws? Not at all! It simply means that all who are in Christ look to Him and trust in Him to be the fulfillment of the law. And, further, being in Christ, we are filled with His love, so:

> Love does no wrong to a neighbor; therefore love is the fulfillment of the Law. (Romans 13:10)

So, I no longer must strive to not steal or covet or to keep the Sabbath. I don't focus on the law or sin; I focus on Christ. Do I still sin? Of course. I'm a WIP after all (work in progress)! But I've also already been forgiven. I am free in Christ—I not only walk by faith, but I also walk by the Spirit:

> But I say, walk by the Spirit, and you will not carry out the desire of the flesh. (Galatians 5:16)

If anyone does follow Old Testament laws because they are told to or because they feel obligated to please God, they are living in legalism. They are not free. They trust their own works more than they trust Christ's work on the cross:

> For by grace you have been saved through faith; and this is not of yourselves, it is the gift of God; not a result of works, so that no one may boast. (Ephesians 2:8-9)

The Israelites spent fifteen hundred years trying to follow the law but failed every day in every way. We try and fail every day too. But Christ's blood covered every sin ever committed. He didn't leave a single sin uncovered. Today, everyone who believes that Jesus died to cover all their sins is now righteous in God's eyes. They are fully forgiven, redeemed, and justified.

We (including Jews!) no longer need to keep dragging sacrificial lambs up to the temple, and we certainly don't need to keep going back to the cross to seek forgiveness for every new sin. We are free in Christ. It is finished!

For Jews, prior to the cross, breaking God's law (the Ten Commandments and the estimated 603 additional laws in the Torah) was sin. And sin required the shedding of blood for it to be forgiven:

> And almost all things are cleansed with blood, according to the Law, and without the shedding of blood there is no forgiveness. (Hebrews 9:22)

With the beginning of Levitical law under Moses, though, the sins of the Israelites were only forgiven by the shedding of blood until they sinned again. While they did hold their annual Day of Atonement for the sins of the nation, there were other sins and situations that required animal sacrifices throughout the year. Israel followed this program for fifteen hundred years! Jesus certainly followed it as well during His thirty-three years on earth. (No, Jesus never sinned, but He would have celebrated the Day of Atonement and every other Jewish festival.)

Israelites in Old Testament times weren't saved from eternity in hell by those animal sacrifices, though. The sacrifices were only a bandage. They never permanently covered sin:

> Under the old covenant, the priest stands and ministers before the altar day after day, offering the same sacrifices again and again, which can never take away sins. (Hebrews 10:11 NLT)

They needed faith in God to be saved, as seen in these two New Testament passages that both reference Genesis 15:6:

> Abraham was, humanly speaking, the founder of our Jewish nation. What did he discover about being made right with God? If his good deeds had made him acceptable to God, he would have had something to boast about. But that was not God's way. For the Scriptures tell us, "Abraham believed God, and God counted him as righteous because of his faith." When people work, their wages are not a gift, but something they have earned. But people are counted as righteous, not because of their work, but because of their faith in God who forgives sinners. (Romans 4:1-5 NLT)

> In the same way, "Abraham believed God, and God counted him as righteous because of his faith." The real children of Abraham, then, are those who put their faith in God. (Galatians 3:6-7 NLT)

While belief saved God's people, He still held them accountable for following the law and the prophets. That would be the program until Jesus was crucified. Something changed while He hung on that cross, though. Consider the words of the thief on the cross next to Him:

> And he was saying, "Jesus, remember me when You come into your kingdom!" And He said to him, "Truly I say to you, today you will be with Me in Paradise." (Luke 23:42-43)

As we know now, Christ's kingdom wouldn't come for at least another two thousand years, so Jesus basically told him, "I'll do something even better for you. Today, I will bring you with Me into Paradise."

Paradise (or Abraham's bosom) was where believers in God went before Christ died. The thief did not go directly to heaven. He would soon enter heaven, though, when Christ Himself ascended there forty-three days later (Ephesians 4:8).

This thief never repented, was never baptized in water for his sins, and certainly wasn't following the law. (Or he wouldn't have been in that situation.) But he did reveal his faith in Jesus, that he believed in Him, that he knew who Jesus was, that He was the Son of God, the Messiah.

His words weren't dramatic or emotional. He didn't repent. And he didn't ask Jesus to forgive him of his sins. He didn't need to. Jesus knew his heart. That is the only way Jesus could have responded with, "Truly I say to you, today you will be with Me in Paradise."

The thief spoke these words from the overflow of his heart—words that revealed his authentic faith and trust in Jesus.

God's program of salvation changed in that moment. While the core had always been by belief and faith in God, Jews *still* had to follow the law and the prophets, they still had to repent and be baptized in water for the forgiveness of their sins.

Even Jesus followed the law and the prophets! He was also baptized in water as if a repentant sinner Himself. And He preached the kingdom gospel throughout His three-year ministry. But... He was about to speak His final words: "It is finished."

With His death, burial, and resurrection, Jesus would fulfill the law and the prophets. That accomplishment then made way for the gospel of the grace of God, by which we are saved today.

Back to Acts
Returning to the book of Acts, we see no patterns for salvation or baptism doctrine. We do, however, see one biblical truth confirmed: salvation comes by *believing alone*. No prayer needed. No prayer of repentance, forgiveness, or salvation is shown anywhere in Acts, nor anywhere in all of scripture.

Therefore, no form of a "sinner's prayer" is biblical. Nowhere does the Bible give us the words for saying a prayer of salvation.

There is certainly nothing at all wrong with saying a prayer, though. Whether by yourself or one led by a pastor or another disciple of Christ.

The danger comes in believing that the words being said are what saves. Words don't save. Only Jesus saves. Only His work on the cross saves us from the consequences of sin—spiritual death and eternity in the lake of fire.

Salvation comes only by believing in the heart that Jesus shed His blood to pay the price for our sins. Not one thing more.

But didn't Paul write in Romans that if we confess with our mouth we will be saved? Yes, but...

Here is what he wrote:

> But what does it say? "The word is near you, in your mouth and in your heart"—that is, the word of faith which we are preaching, that if you confess with your mouth Jesus as Lord, and believe in your heart that God raised Him from the dead, you will be saved;

> for with the heart a person believes, resulting in righteousness, and with the mouth he confesses, resulting in salvation. (Romans 10:8-10)

Paul was not adding works to salvation. He was also not contradicting the gospel of salvation Jesus gave to him (1 Corinthians 15:1-4). That's not what's going on here.

In 1 Corinthians 15, Paul made no mention of professing Christ as Lord for salvation. We are still saved solely by the grace of God alone through faith alone (Ephesians 2:8-9).

We have seen, and will continue to see, that salvation today is not by *any* work on our part, including by any words we might say or by making Jesus our Lord. He is *already* Lord. We don't need to do or say anything to formally *make* Him Lord. And we certainly don't need to confess Him as Lord as a requirement for our salvation.

Throughout Romans 10, Paul stressed over and over that salvation is based on belief (faith) alone, including in verses 4, 6, 8-11, and 14.

Confession does not bring salvation, only faith does.

Paul did write in Romans 10:10, "... and with the mouth he confesses, resulting in salvation." This does not mean that confession is a condition of salvation, though. It can't be, because that would be a work on our part, to confess Christ as Lord. And here is what Paul wrote in the very next verse:

> For the Scripture says, "Whoever believes in Him will not be put to shame." (Romans 10:11)

Salvation is by faith alone.

So, what did Paul mean with these verses? Simply that confession is a natural result or fruit of salvation, not a condition of it. A person does not confess Christ in order *to be saved*; he confesses Christ *because he is saved*. Just like the thief on the cross, we confess Christ from the overflow of our heart, which is exactly where belief in Christ comes from.

To be clear: Confession doesn't save, it advances the gospel. It preaches. This is what Paul told us in the verses that follow:

> How then are they to call on Him in whom they have not believed? How are they to believe in Him whom they have not heard? And how are they to hear without a preacher? But how are they to preach unless they are sent? Just as it is written: "How beautiful are the feet of those who bring good news of good things!" (Romans 10:14-15)

So, the context of confession is evangelism, not salvation. Paul was especially encouraging his fellow Jews to confess Christ as Savior to see more of them be saved. Jews believed in a coming Messiah, but most didn't (and still don't) believe that *Jesus was* that promised Messiah!

Paul cared deeply about the salvation of all people, both Jew and Gentile:

> For I am not ashamed of the gospel, for it is the power of God for salvation to everyone who believes, to the Jew first and also to the Greek. (Romans 1:16)

I am not saying that believers shouldn't call Jesus their Lord, because we all should. I am only saying that we shouldn't call Him Lord or make Him Lord *as a work* for salvation.

Just like the lowly thief on the cross, Abraham too was made righteous by believing, though four thousand years earlier. And what made Abraham and the thief righteous still makes us righteous today:

> And He took him outside and said, "Now look toward the heavens and count the stars, if you are able to count them." And He said to him, "So shall your descendants be." Then he believed in the Lord; and He credited it to him as righteousness. (Genesis 15:5-6)

Paul exposed the danger of the sinner's prayer. Really any prayer of salvation. They are just words unless the heart agrees and proves to God that the belief is authentic. If the heart doesn't believe, the words don't matter.

The gospel message by which we're saved today—the grace of God through faith in the blood of Jesus—does not appear anywhere in the book of Acts, nor in the gospels of Matthew, Mark, Luke, or John. Further, neither Jesus nor His disciples ever talked about the grace of God as the way of salvation.

What's going on here?

A transition.

From law to grace. And here again is the proof directly from Paul himself, who alone received these revelations from God:

> For by grace you have been saved through faith; and this is not of yourselves, it is the gift of God; not a result of works, so that no one may boast. (Ephesians 2:8-9)
>
> Let me now remind you, dear brothers and sisters, of the Good News I preached to you before. You welcomed it then, and you still stand firm in it. It is this Good News that saves you if you continue to believe the message I told you—unless, of course, you believed something that was never true in the first place. I passed on to you what was most important and what had also been passed on to me. Christ died for our sins, just as the Scriptures said. He was buried, and he was raised from the dead on the third day, just as the Scriptures said. (1 Corinthians 15:1-4 NLT)

As you see, Paul tells us that "this Good News that saves" is believing "Christ died for our sins… was buried… and raised from the dead on the third day."

This is the only gospel that saves today.

The gospel that Jesus and John the Baptist preached (and the disciples for most of their lives) was not the same gospel that Jesus revealed to Paul. They preached the gospel of the kingdom to Jews, while Paul preached the gospel of grace initially to Jews and then to Gentiles.

Jesus was sent to the Jews first in His earthly ministry. God's ultimate plan, though, was to save all people of all nations. He simply chose the line of Abraham, Isaac, and Jacob (Israel) to be the people through which the Savior of the world would come.

These are both gospels of Jesus Christ: the one that Jesus and His disciples preached to Jews, and the one that Paul preached, which he received directly from Jesus:

> Dear brothers and sisters, I want you to understand that the gospel message I preach is not based on mere human reasoning. I received my message from no human source, and no one taught me. Instead, I received it by direct revelation from Jesus Christ. (Galatians 1:11-12 NLT)

Peter and the other apostles slowly got on board with this gospel of grace, but it was Paul, Barnabas, Timothy, Titus, and others who took it to the Gentiles, not the disciples of Jesus.

Referring to Table 1, salvation today is an individual's first experience, before either water or Spirit baptism. Spirit baptisms did not always happen in Acts or were not always recorded. Or if they did happen, they occurred later, possibly weeks, months, or even years later.

Here are the major issues that have led to contention and confusion from within the book of Acts:

- The order of salvations, water baptisms, and Spirit baptisms are not consistent.

- Spirit baptisms occurred three different ways: initiated by God or Jesus, by a disciple's prayer, and by a disciple laying hands on the recipient.

- God opened salvation up to Gentiles (*all* people), not just Jews.

As well, many transitions occurred throughout the period covering the book of Acts. Here are a few of them:

- Jews went from needing repentance and water baptism for forgiveness of sins (before Jesus died) to only needing water baptism in the name of the Lord Jesus…
- … to later believing in the death, burial, and resurrection of Jesus alone for salvation.
- Samaritans—despised by Jews because they were part Jew and part pagan—were welcomed into God's program of salvation (John 4:9). (#4 in Table 1)
- After Christ's resurrection, salvation occurred first, *before* water baptism, and never by any words spoken, including a prayer.
- Jews who were water-baptized by John the Baptist, a disciple of his, or a disciple of Jesus needed to be water-baptized *again* after Christ's resurrection and ascension. (#11)
- These same Jews also needed to hear that there was a Holy Spirit and receive Him/be baptized in Him. (#11)
- After Christ's resurrection, salvations occurred by *hearing* the gospel message being proclaimed and responding with the heart.
- Gentiles were now welcomed into God's program of salvation, much to the surprise (and disdain) of some apostles and other Jewish believers. (#7)

- Gentiles go from pagan-worshipping people far from God to being saved and receiving the Holy Spirit *first*, followed by water baptism. (#7, 8, 9)

- Water baptism is no longer necessary for repentance, forgiveness of sins, or salvation after Christ was crucified. That was God's program for pre-resurrection Jews only.

- Apostleship moved from Jesus's disciples/apostles to Paul and his disciples.

- The focus also shifted unmistakably from Peter to Paul. (No mention of Peter after Acts 15.)

From Table 1, we see that Jews who had been baptized into John's baptism (whether by John the Baptist himself or another disciple) could not have been saved by grace through faith in the blood because: 1) Christ had not yet shed His blood for all mankind, and 2) the message of salvation by grace was revealed *only* to Paul many years after John the Baptist was killed and Jesus had ascended.

In Acts 8, we see that Simon (a Samaritan and sorcerer) was "saved." However, he immediately proved that his conversion was not sincere. He faked it. His heart was not "right before God" (Acts 8:18-24).

This is further proof that salvation is an act of the heart (believing) versus any words we might say. Words can be deceiving, but God knows the heart:

> Every person's way is right in his own eyes,
> But the Lord examines the hearts. (Proverbs 21:2)

> And He [Jesus] said to them, "You are the ones who justify yourselves in the sight of people, but God knows your hearts; because that which is highly esteemed among people is detestable in the sight of God." (Luke 16:15)

Also, note that for Cornelius and his household (#7), Peter preached the gospel to them (Acts 10:34-43, especially verses 39-40). The gospel he preached, though, that led to their salvation was that Jesus died on a cross and "God raised Him up on the third day."

If we compare what Peter preached to that Gentile household and what Paul tells us is the gospel that saves today, Peter did not include the phrase "Christ died for our sins." The disciples did not yet understand that Jesus shed His blood to wash away sin. But in that moment, these Gentiles believed what Christ had done for them and God saved them. How is this possible?

Because God had not yet revealed to Paul the gospel message of salvation by grace through faith in the blood of Jesus—again, as seen in 1 Corinthians 15:1-4. God could not hold anyone accountable for the gospel of grace if He hadn't revealed it yet.

Acts 10:44 then says:

> While Peter was still speaking these words, the Holy Spirit fell upon all those who were listening to the message.

Notice that these new Gentile believers were then baptized with the power of the Holy Spirit *without saying a word!* They didn't say a prayer, nor did Peter lead them in a prayer (he was still preaching), nor did he pray over them to receive Jesus as their Savior, nor did he baptize them in the Holy Spirit. None of this happened. He just proclaimed to them what he witnessed about Jesus; they heard, believed, and were saved. God, Jesus, and the Holy Spirit did all the work!

Peter didn't know what to do, so he just talked about Jesus. The Gentiles simply listened and believed. Nothing fancy. No slideshow. No altar call. No raising of hands. No prayer. No soft, emotional music playing in the background. No light show. No fake smoke rolling up from the floor.

Though Luke didn't record every detail for us, we can easily work out the order of events. This family of Gentiles *anticipated* something special, maybe even supernatural, when Cornelius, head of the household, sent for Peter. (As seen in Acts 10:1-23, God had given Peter and Cornelius each a separate vision, and they both obeyed what God told them to do.)

Cornelius and his household certainly would have already heard about Jesus and were prepared to hear some "Good News." As Peter was talking about Jesus, they *believed in their hearts* the words he spoke, that Jesus was put to death and God raised Him up on the third day. *Then* the Holy Spirit fell on them.

These Gentiles were saved first (by believing in their heart that Jesus died and God raised Him up), then Spirit-baptized, and finally baptized in water. Know that Peter baptized them in water not because it was part of God's salvation program, but because that was what Jews did! It's all he knew to do. He was going to continue doing what he knew to do, even for Gentiles. No one had told him anything different.

Finally, in Table 1, you will see that the Jewish disciples Paul met at Ephesus (#11) had only experienced the baptism of John the Baptist. They had not been baptized in the name of Jesus and had not received the Spirit baptism. Paul gave them some exciting news:

> Paul said, "John baptized with a baptism of repentance, telling the people to believe in Him who was coming after him, that is, in Jesus." (Acts 19:4)

Paul was telling them, "Things have changed! Jesus did come. So, there's been a transition since John baptized you." Here's how these men responded:

> When they heard this, they were baptized in the name of the Lord Jesus. And when Paul had laid hands upon them, the Holy Spirit came on them and they began speaking with tongues and prophesying. There were about twelve men in all. (Acts 19:5-7)

John's baptism was only meant to prepare the hearts of the Jewish people for their coming Messiah. Through his ministry, Jews were to repent—change their mind about their relationship with God and who Jesus was—and be water-baptized.

These water baptisms didn't save them, though, nor did they give them the indwelling of the Holy Spirit (who had not yet come because Christ had not yet ascended to the Father in heaven), nor did they give them the Spirit baptism.

Paul's preaching to these Jews in Ephesus got them saved, baptized in water in the name of the Lord Jesus, and baptized with the Holy Spirit.

(Note: We don't yet see Paul preaching a message of salvation by grace through faith in the blood of Jesus. We don't know if he hadn't yet received this revelation from God or if he'd received it but not yet revealed it to anyone. He didn't write 1 Corinthians until three or four years later, which, as we've seen, includes the gospel of salvation in 15:1-4.)

As you can see, we would (and do) create serious misunderstandings and arguments if we pull doctrine from the book of Acts—what we believe and teach and how we behave in churches and as the Body of Christ. This is especially true regarding salvation and baptisms. There is just too much inconsistency and disparity in the transition from the Old Testament's law and prophets to what God intended for this current age of grace and for the church, the Body of Christ.

Acts is solely a book of transition and history. We should read it, understand it, learn from it, and enjoy it, but not pull doctrine from it.

It is certainly still scripture and therefore God-inspired, inerrant, and infallible. Paul tells us that *all* scripture is beneficial for us:

> All Scripture is inspired by God and beneficial for teaching, for rebuke, for correction, for training in righteousness; so that the man or woman of God may be fully capable, equipped for every good work. (2 Timothy 3:16-17)

But we need to rightly divide the Word of God—to use every verse and passage only as God intended, not to decide for ourselves which verses to use for doctrine, which to use for rebuke or correction or training in righteousness. This is exactly what Paul made clear in 2 Timothy 2:15:

> Be diligent to present yourself approved to God as a worker who does not need to be ashamed, **accurately handling the word of truth**.

Paul was telling Pastor Timothy (and therefore us) that if he faithfully applied the right scriptures for the right situations, then he never had to be ashamed of what he preached or what he taught or what others said about him because he was honoring God by accurately handling His Word for the benefit of the Body of Christ.

What Really Happened at Pentecost?

Pentecost is an essential event to explore when discussing Spirit baptisms. The more we understand what really happened at that festival in AD 30, the clearer Spirit baptisms become as a biblical truth for today.

In this section, we'll clarify what happened and what didn't happen, as well as provide some cool insights to know about that most amazing day in both Jewish and Christian history.

Pentecost is a wonderful overlap of Jewish and Christian celebrations. Jews, of course, don't celebrate Pentecost as it relates to the arrival of the Holy Spirit, but they do celebrate Pentecost, or what they call Shavuot.

Shavuot is one of three festivals that required Jewish men to travel to Jerusalem and observe the festival at the Holy Temple. This feast is also called the Festival of Harvest, the Day of First Fruits, and the Festival of Weeks.

For Jews, Shavuot is celebrated fifty days after the first day of Passover. Passover commemorates the night the Israelites fled Egypt, before which God directed them to apply the blood of a slain lamb to their doorposts so the angel of death would "pass over" their home, protecting them from God's wrath destined for the Egyptians (Exodus 12:1-13).

Shavuot itself is the festival where Jews commemorate Moses receiving the gift of the Torah from God on Mount Sinai (Exodus 20:1-17), which included the Ten Commandments—the Torah being the first five books of the Old Testament, as mentioned earlier.

For Christians, we celebrate Pentecost as the day God sent the promised Holy Spirit after Jesus ascended to heaven:

> I will ask the Father, and He will give you another Helper, so that He may be with you forever; the Helper is the Spirit of truth, whom the world cannot receive, because it does not see Him or know Him; but you know Him because He remains with you and will be in you. (John 14:16-17)

Jerusalem would have been packed with tens of thousands of people celebrating Shavuot. Acts 2:5 tells us they traveled from "every nation under heaven," and verses 9-11 list fifteen different nations from which men journeyed.

Jews in attendance that day were celebrating this very special feast. They certainly weren't expecting anything out of the ordinary or supernatural to happen. That included the disciples, who had returned to Jerusalem as Jesus directed them and were doing all they knew to do—hanging out in the upper room, likely sad and demoralized that Jesus was no longer with them.

But, while in the upper room, those 120 disciples heard a "noise like a violent rushing wind" come from above (Acts 2:2). Tongues of fire appeared and distributed upon each of them. They were all *filled* with the Holy Spirit and began to speak with different tongues (known languages) as the Holy Spirit gave them ability.

Festival attendees, alarmed by the noise, ran to see what was happening. They heard the disciples speaking in each of their own native languages! Languages the disciples had *never* learned. They were speaking "the mighty deeds of God" (Acts 2:11).

Then Peter, filled with the power of the Holy Spirit, began preaching. He preached a sermon he hadn't prepared—one he didn't even know he was going to preach. And he preached it in a manner far beyond his country-bumpkin abilities.

Peter had changed. This Peter was bold. Fearless. His preaching was clear and impactful.

The old Peter was afraid. He had denied His Savior three times. And he spent the last few weeks hiding from the Jewish rulers in the upper room.

As Jesus promised, His Father sent another Helper, and the Helper fell on the disciples with the full power of God. This was their immersion with the Holy Spirit. This was a totally different baptism than when Jesus breathed the Holy Spirit into them just before His ascension (John 20:22).

That experience didn't empower Peter or the other disciples. This one did.

Believers today receive the indwelling of the Holy Spirit at their salvation. We need a separate event just like the disciples experienced to have the Holy Spirit come upon us with power. That is the baptism in (or with) the Holy Spirit.

Facts about the Day of Pentecost in Acts 2:

- Tens of thousands would have been in Jerusalem and witnessed the event.

- The disciples spoke in known languages they had never learned (verse 8).
- Attendees heard the disciples speak in their own native languages (verse 8).
- Christ's death was *God's* plan (verse 23).
- Christ's resurrection was God's plan as well (verse 24).
- About three thousand souls were saved that day (verse 41).
- All those in attendance and saved were Jews (verse 22).
- Jesus's prophecy of the Holy Spirit arriving was fulfilled (John 14:16).
- John the Baptist and Joel's prophecies were also fulfilled:

As for me, I baptize you with water for repentance, but He who is coming after me is mightier than I, and I am not fit to remove His sandals; He will baptize you with the Holy Spirit and fire. (Matthew 3:11)

It will come about after this
That I will pour out My Spirit **on all mankind**;
And your sons and your daughters will prophesy,
Your old men will have dreams,
Your young men will see visions.
And even on the male and female servants

> I will pour out My Spirit in those days.
> (Joel 2:28-29)

Pentecost: What Didn't Happen

To clear up misunderstandings, here are three things that *did not* happen that miraculous Day of Pentecost—and are *not* supported by scripture.

No Indwelling of the Holy Spirit

The disciples *did not* receive their indwelling of the Holy Spirit at Pentecost because, as mentioned in the previous section, they had already received that indwelling in John 20:22. *This event at Pentecost was a fully separate experience for them—the Holy Spirit coming upon them with power.*

All believers receive the indwelling of the Holy Spirit the moment of their salvation (1 Corinthians 12:13). As with the disciples at Pentecost, believers can also receive a separate *baptism with the Holy Spirit*.

No Doctrine Established

In line with the first part of this chapter, no doctrine was intended or established at Pentecost. This is especially true regarding speaking in tongues as being the initial evidence of baptism in the Holy Spirit. No scripture supports this notion.

Billions of people have been saved since the crucifixion of Christ, and many of those have also been baptized in the Holy Spirit. But not all received a private prayer language.

I was saved and water-baptized for thirty-six years and never experienced speaking in tongues. But within a few months of my Spirit baptism, I began speaking in tongues without any effort on my part.

Further, Paul gives us three clear verses that contradict the notion of speaking in tongues as the evidence of baptism in the Holy Spirit:

> All do not have gifts of healings, do they? All do not speak with tongues, do they? All do not interpret, do they? (1 Corinthians 12:30)

> Now I wish that you all spoke in tongues, but rather that you would prophesy; and greater is the one who prophesies than the one who speaks in tongues, unless he interprets, so that the church may receive edification. (1 Corinthians 14:5)

> Therefore, my brothers and sisters, earnestly desire to prophesy, and do not forbid speaking in tongues. But all things must be done properly and in an orderly way. (1 Corinthians 14:39-40)

Those who exalt speaking in tongues ignore what the apostle Paul teaches. He did not even emphasize speaking in tongues, but prophesying—*four times*! Regarding tongues, he simply said he wished everyone spoke in tongues but not to forbid others from doing it, adding that it "must be done properly and in an orderly way."

There are only three occasions in scripture where speaking in tongues reveals evidence of baptism in the Holy Spirit. All three occur in the book of Acts. None are in Paul's writings.

Yet there are many examples throughout Acts where speaking in tongues *does not* happen after baptism in the Holy Spirit.

Pentecost: Two Amazing Things to Know
1) The Day of First Fruits

As previously discussed, Shavuot (Pentecost) was one of three Jewish festivals observed at the Holy Temple in Jerusalem. Another name for Shavuot is the Day of First Fruits. It is celebrated fifty days after the first day of Passover, which commemorates when God saved the Israelites from death because they applied the blood of a slain lamb to their doorposts.

The Day of First Fruits was originally celebrated when the Israelites entered the Promised Land and God directed them to give the first of their harvest to Him—a harvest *He* provided. He had already proven His faithfulness by providing manna and water throughout their forty years in the wilderness.

Just like those innocent lambs slain at the first Passover, Jesus's death also took place on Passover. God then raised Him to life three days later. Because of this, Jesus became the "first fruits" of all who would die spiritually and be raised to new life in Him:

> But the fact is, Christ has been raised from the dead, the first fruits of those who are asleep. (1 Corinthians 15:20)

Just as the Israelites were saved by the blood of a slain lamb at the first Passover, we, too, are saved by the blood of a slain Lamb at Passover. God gave the first and best of all He had—His innocent Son.

Christ became the "first fruits" when God raised Him from the dead. His resurrection produced a bounty that Day of Pentecost when three thousand souls were saved. And that was just the beginning of what He accomplished on the cross. Through the work of the Holy Spirit, He continues to add to that bounty every day, even two thousand years later.

Here is how Jesus Himself described what He would do (and did) on the cross:

> Truly, truly I say to you, unless a grain of wheat falls into the earth and dies, it remains alone; but if it dies, it bears much fruit. (John 12:24)

It was necessary for Jesus to die so that you and I could live. He did fall into the earth (grave) and die for you and me. His death produced a bounty of fruit—our salvation and the salvation of billions of people who have put their faith in Him for six thousand years.

Through His resurrection, Christ became the *"first fruits"* of all who would experience spiritual death but then be raised again to new life.

2) Reversing Babel

Genesis 11:1-9 gives us the interesting story of the tower of Babel. Acts 2 gives us the story of Pentecost. As with much of God's Word, these two stories appear unrelated, but God tightly wove them together.

He used Pentecost in AD 30 to reverse what He had done at the tower of Babel over twenty-two hundred years earlier.

In those days, people of the earth spoke just one language. "We" humans were getting too smart and arrogant for our own good. Since all humans spoke just one language, someone came up with a super idea:

> And they said, "Come, let's build ourselves a city, and a tower whose top will reach into heaven, and let's make a name for ourselves; otherwise we will be scattered abroad over the face of all the earth." (Genesis 11:4)

But God heard what was happening and paid a visit to Babel:

> And the Lord said, "Behold, they are one people, and they all have the same language. And this is what they have started to do, and now nothing which they plan to do will be impossible for them. Come, let Us go down and there confuse their language, so that they will not understand one another's speech." So the Lord scattered them abroad from there over the face of all the earth; and they stopped building the city. Therefore it was named Babel, because there the Lord confused the language of all the earth; and from there the Lord scattered them abroad over the face of all the earth. (Genesis 11:6-9)

When the Day of Pentecost arrived, God needed to make sure the Good News of His Son's life, death, burial, and resurrection spread around the world. But He had confused the language of men and dispersed them. He was now ready to reverse or "fulfill" what He'd done at Babel, once again permitting mankind to communicate so that this Good News could be shared.

He accomplished this at Pentecost by sending His Holy Spirit *upon* the disciples as if "tongues of fire." The disciples could now supernaturally speak in languages they never learned.

God reversed what He had done at the tower of Babel. He had removed the ability of men to communicate for their own earthly purposes but then restored their ability to communicate for His heavenly purposes. Mankind tried using its own human spirit and effort to reach up to God. Instead, at Pentecost, God used His Son and Holy Spirit to reach down to us.

God used this supernatural "tongues" ability to jump-start the spread of the gospel of Jesus Christ. The thousands of Jews saved that Day of Pentecost would then return to their own nations and share the Good News that changed their lives.

Outline of the Book of Acts

In this final section of Chapter 4, I simply provide a brief outline of each chapter in the book of Acts. The twenty-eight chapters divide perfectly into four segments of seven chapters each. This is my perspective of Acts, a way to provide a high-level understanding of the book and the flow of events as God transitioned the world from His age of the law and prophets to His age of grace and the church.

*The Holy Spirit arrives at Pentecost and the
disciples are empowered to preach.
(Note: Acts 1–7 was written about Jews and to Jews.)*

- Chapter 1: Jesus's ascension to heaven; Matthias chosen to replace Judas Iscariot.

- Chapter 2: Pentecost—Holy Spirit enters as wind/fire; Peter preaches, and three thousand Jews are saved.

- Chapter 3: Peter heals a lame man, then preaches his second sermon and five thousand Jews are saved.

- Chapter 4: Religious leaders arrest Peter and John, and they are warned not to preach again.

- Chapter 5: Ananias and Sapphira fall dead for lying to the Holy Spirit; apostles imprisoned.

- Chapter 6: Seven disciples chosen as caretakers of church members, including Stephen.

- Chapter 7: Stephen preaches to Jewish leaders and then they stone him to death, with Saul (Paul) watching in support.

God begins His transition from Jews to Gentiles.

- Chapter 8: Philip preaches in Samaria, then to an Ethiopian eunuch (a proselyte to Judaism).

- Chapter 9: Jesus confronts, converts, and calls Saul of Tarsus on the road to Damascus.

Chapter 10: God sends Peter to Caesarea via a dream; first Gentiles converted.

Chapter 11: The disciples complain to Peter about preaching to Gentiles; first "Christians" in Antioch.

Chapter 12: Peter's arrest and miraculous deliverance from prison.

Chapter 13: Paul takes his first missionary journey; Jews reject him, so he goes to Gentiles.

Chapter 14: Paul in Lystra, where he is stoned by Jews and left for dead.

Peter begins to understand Paul's gospel of salvation by grace through faith alone; Paul expands the Christian church into Europe.

Chapter 15: The council at Jerusalem: agreement to limit Jewish law placed on Gentile Christians.

Chapter 16: Paul's second missionary journey; Lydia is the first convert in Europe; Paul in prison.

Chapter 17: Paul in Thessalonica, Berea, and Athens, including his sermon on Mars Hill.

Chapter 18: Paul in Corinth, where he receives a message from Jesus; third missionary journey.

Chapter 19: Paul in Ephesus; miracles.

Chapter 20: Paul in Macedonia and Greece; Jews plot to kill him.

Chapter 21: Paul in Jerusalem, where he's seized by the Jews.

Paul continues to defend and fight for the Christian faith while in prison and facing death.

Chapter 22: Paul tells his story of conversion to Jewish leaders; they threaten to kill him.

Chapter 23: Paul again before the Jewish council defending himself; Jews plot to kill him.

Chapter 24: Paul put on trial; Jews falsely accuse him, then imprison him.

Chapter 25: Paul on trial again; appeals to Caesar; third trial in front of King Agrippa.

Chapter 26: Paul defends himself before King Agrippa.

Chapter 27: Paul sent to Rome to defend himself to Caesar; shipwrecked on the way.

Chapter 28: Paul shipwrecked on Malta, snakebit, imprisoned in Rome.

More about Paul

As a Pharisee, the apostle Paul was originally a brutal persecutor of Jews who were turning to Christ:

> But Saul began ravaging the church, entering house after house; and he would drag away men and women and put them in prison. (Acts 8:3)

(Note: The word "church" here was *not* referring to a "Christian" church at that time. It couldn't be. The Koine Greek word used here for "church" is *ekklésia* and means a gathering, assembly, or congregation. It simply refers to a group of people that have been "called out." Think of the Israelites being called out of Egypt. *Ekklésia* was also used in Acts 19:32 to refer to the assembled mob wanting to harm Paul. That certainly wasn't a church! Here, in Acts 8:3, though, it indicates the broad assembly of Jewish believers in Christ at that time. The Christian church is more accurately called the Body of Christ, and the Body did not begin until Jesus revealed it to Paul sometime after his conversion on the road to Damascus.)

Once a brutal hunter of Jewish believers in Christ, Paul became the hunted. With the tables turned, Paul began to be brutally persecuted himself by Jews and would be throughout his roughly thirty years of ministry. But he understood it:

> But in everything commending ourselves as servants of God, in much endurance, in afflictions, in hardships, in difficulties, in beatings, in imprisonments, in mob attacks, in labors, in sleeplessness, in hunger, in purity, in knowledge, in patience, in kindness, in the Holy Spirit, in genuine love, in the word of truth, and in the power of God; by the weapons of righteousness for the right hand and the left, by glory and dishonor, by evil report and good report; regarded as deceivers

and yet true; as unknown and yet well known, as dying and yet behold, we are alive; as punished and yet not put to death, as sorrowful yet always rejoicing, as poor yet making many rich, as having nothing and yet possessing all things. (2 Corinthians 6:4-10)

Through it all, Paul never stopped giving all glory to his Lord and Savior, Jesus Christ. He never stopped fighting for the faith until his death. And through his letters, he continues to fight the good fight of faith and pour into believers throughout the world.

Now, with this deeper understanding of the events in the book of Acts, let's dive into the core chapters of this book and discover the three baptisms of Jesus, His disciples, and believers today.

CORE CHAPTERS

5

The Three Baptisms of Jesus

SCRIPTURE RECORDS VERY clearly and without question that Jesus experienced three baptisms:

1. Water baptism: baptized in water by John the Baptist
2. Spirit baptism: baptized with the Holy Spirit by His Father
3. Cross or grave baptism: baptized (immersed) into death by His Father

As you can see, Jesus didn't experience a "salvation" or "conversion" baptism as we do. So, before we look at the purpose and meaning of each of Christ's baptisms, let's first understand why Jesus didn't need to be saved. This may seem obvious, but deeper reasons exist, which will have you appreciating God the Father and your Savior even more.

Jesus Didn't Need to Be Saved

Jesus was, is, and always will be without sin. Instead of needing salvation, He *is* our salvation. As we learned in Chapter 1, only those who have sinned need to be saved. That's pretty much everyone who's ever lived… except Jesus.

> For all have sinned and fall short of the glory of God. (Romans 3:23)

We all descend from Adam and so are born of the bloodline of Adam. That means *everyone*, unfortunately, inherits his sinful nature.

Adam sinned by disobeying God. (Eve was only deceived.) That got him and Eve kicked out of Eden. That one sin also separated them both from God physically and spiritually, setting physical death in their future as well. Because we are the offspring of Adam, we, too, are born with a sin nature that separates us from God:

> But your wrongdoings have caused a separation between you and your God,
> And your sins have hidden His face from you so that He does not hear. (Isaiah 59:2)

> When Adam sinned, sin entered the world. Adam's sin brought death, so death spread to everyone, for everyone sinned. (Romans 5:12 NLT)

All humans need salvation—to be set free from the bondage of sin and made right with God. But to be made right with

God requires us to be made perfect, unblemished, without sin. That can only happen if we are redeemed—bought at a price. Only then can we once again be in proper relationship with our Father in heaven.

Jesus Christ is our redemption because God purchased us at the price of His innocent Son's life:

> For you have been bought for a price: therefore glorify God in your body. (1 Corinthians 6:20)

> In Him we have redemption through His blood, the forgiveness of our wrongdoings, according to the riches of His grace. (Ephesians 1:7)

We also need salvation so that we can enter His presence in heaven, for God does not allow sin in heaven:

> And nothing unclean, and no one who practices abomination and lying, shall ever come into it, but only those whose names are written in the Lamb's book of life. (Revelation 21:27)

If Jesus had sinned just once, He could never have died for our sins. God would not have allowed it. Instead, God would have required Him to die for His own sins. He requires this of us as well. But the Good News is, Jesus lived and died a perfect life, spotless, without sin. Therefore, God chose to sacrifice His only Son on the cross so that we might live:

> For we do not have a high priest who cannot sympathize with our weaknesses, but One who has been tempted in all things just as we are, yet without sin. (Hebrews 4:15)

> It was the precious blood of Christ, the sinless, spotless Lamb of God. (1 Peter 1:19 NLT)

> For if while we were enemies we were reconciled to God through the death of His Son, much more, having been reconciled, we shall be saved by His life. (Romans 5:10)

God has always required blood to be shed to atone for sin:

> In fact, according to the law of Moses, nearly everything was purified with blood. For without the shedding of blood, there is no forgiveness. (Hebrews 9:22 NLT)

But the regular sacrificing of animals in the temple would never be enough to cover every human's sins. Jesus shed His blood for us once and for all! *One* time for *all* humans for *all* sins for *all* time:

> And he did not enter heaven to offer himself again and again, like the high priest here on earth who enters the Most Holy Place year after year with the blood of an animal. If that had been necessary, Christ would have had to die again and again, ever since the world

began. But now, once for all time, he has appeared at the end of the age to remove sin by his own death as a sacrifice. (Hebrews 9:25-26 NLT)

Under the old covenant, the high priest would enter the temple's Most Holy Place one day each year (on Yom Kippur, the Day of Atonement). He would apply the blood of a bull and goat on the cover of the ark of the covenant, which held the stone tablets of the Ten Commandments. But Jesus's death forever ended that old, insufficient, unsustainable way of atoning for sin:

> With his own blood—not the blood of goats and calves—he entered the Most Holy Place once for all time and secured our redemption forever. (Hebrews 9:12 NLT)

Jesus never sinned. He was perfect. Therefore, He *could not* have been born of man, of the bloodline of Adam. And He wasn't. He was born of God the Father through the Holy Spirit:

> Now the birth of Jesus the Messiah was as follows: when His mother Mary had been betrothed to Joseph, before they came together she was found to be pregnant by the Holy Spirit. (Matthew 1:18)

Jesus entered the world perfect and remained perfect through His death on the cross. That is the *only* way that God the Father could allow Him to die for us—as the perfect, spotless, innocent lamb:

> Whatever has a defect, you shall not offer, for it will not be accepted for you. (Leviticus 22:20)

> He made Him who knew no sin to be sin in our behalf, so that we might become the righteousness of God in Him. (2 Corinthians 5:21)

Do you see how desperately God loves you? How He not only made a way to bring you back into His presence, but desires for you to return to Him? He sent His innocent Son to die on a cross for you so that you could be forever forgiven and forever free. You only need to believe that Jesus died for you.

Three Baptisms

Now let's dive into the three baptisms of Jesus:

1) Water Baptism

Jesus was first baptized in water. His cousin, John the Baptist, reluctantly performed it (Matthew 3:13-17; Mark 1:9-11; Luke 3:21-22).

I love letting the scene of Jesus's baptism in the Jordan River unfold in my mind:

John, watching excitedly as Jesus approaches him, then anxious and perplexed when Jesus asks John to baptize Him. John pushes back against Jesus's request, but then agrees. When Jesus comes up out of the water, the Holy Spirit immediately descends on Him like a dove floating down. God the Father speaks from heaven—and *all* in attendance can hear Him: "This is My Son, in whom I am well pleased."

It truly is one of the most awe-inspiring scenes in the Bible. It's such a beautiful display of the Trinity at work on earth and from heaven, with heaven coming to earth in the form of the Holy Spirit.

In the story, we see God the Father, God the Son, and God the Holy Spirit uniquely revealing themselves to the world—the Father's love for His Son, the Son's humility of receiving water baptism, and the Holy Spirit descending and remaining on the Son.

I wonder if His passion—three years in the future—slid through His mind during His baptism: His full weight hanging on His cousin John's arms as He surrendered to His death. Then fully submerged face-up, as if already lying lifeless in the tomb. And, finally, bursting from the water to new life, paralleling His triumphant resurrection three days later.

There's even more to this beautiful, supernatural scene than most realize, especially how it connects the Old Testament to the New Testament, but also how it further shifts God's plan of salvation from old covenant law to new covenant grace through His Son's death.

Christ's water baptism initiated His earthly ministry, while His Spirit baptism empowered Him for that ministry. His water baptism also revealed to the world that He came as a lowly human while at the same time fulfilling His required anointing.

Everyone at the Jordan River that day witnessed it. They witnessed Him—Jesus in all His humanity and humility being baptized in water as if a common sinner. They would all soon understand (but not all would believe) that here was the Christ, the Son of God, their long-awaited Messiah.

God had sent John the Baptist ahead of Jesus to the Jewish nation to prepare their hearts and preach a message of repentance and water baptism for the forgiveness of sins:

> Just as it is written in Isaiah the prophet:
>
> "Behold, I am sending My messenger before You,
> Who will prepare Your way;
> The voice of one calling out in the wilderness,
> 'Prepare the way of the LORD,
> Make His paths straight!'"
>
> John the Baptist appeared in the wilderness, preaching a baptism of repentance for the forgiveness of sins. (Mark 1:2-4)

This was the kingdom message that both he and Jesus would preach to the Jews: Repent—change your mind about the path you're on, the path away from God. Instead, turn from your sinful ways, return to God, and be baptized for the forgiveness of your sins.

Of course, Jesus didn't need to repent and turn back to God—He was God! He also didn't need to be baptized in water for the forgiveness of sins.

So, why would Jesus compel John to baptize Him?

John wondered the same thing:

> But John tried to prevent Him, saying, "I have the need to be baptized by You, and yet You are coming to me?" (Matthew 3:14)

Jesus understood something that John didn't:

But Jesus, answering, said to him, "Allow it at this time; for in this way it is fitting for us to fulfill all righteousness." Then he allowed Him. (Matthew 3:15)

What did Jesus mean by, "it is fitting for us to fulfill all righteousness"? What was He up to? Righteousness means to be in right standing with God. Thus, Jesus needed to be baptized in water so He would be in right standing with His Father. Put more bluntly, Jesus had John baptize Him in water because God required it. But for what reason?

To be:

- *Identified* with sinners.
- *Revealed* as the Messiah.
- *Anointed* as High Priest.

Identified with Sinners

Even though Jesus never sinned, He chose to be baptized in water and therefore take on the likeness of a sinner. In preparation for His ministry, God sent John the Baptist to lead his fellow Jews to both repentance and water baptism for the forgiveness of their sins. So, Jesus, as a devout Jew, followed His Father's command and had John baptize Him.

But Jesus went far beyond simply being baptized in water in the likeness of a sinner. He further humbled Himself and *became sin* on our behalf, as we saw in the previous section:

> He made Him who knew no sin to be sin in our behalf, so that we might become the righteousness of God in Him. (2 Corinthians 5:21)

> Though he was God, he did not think of equality with God as something to cling to. Instead, he gave up his divine privileges; he took the humble position of a slave and was born as a human being. When he appeared in human form, he humbled himself in obedience to God and died a criminal's death on a cross. (Philippians 2:6-8 NLT)

Revealed as the Messiah

Jesus did not need to repent or turn from sin, so His baptism was a sign to John that he could *reveal* Jesus as the Son of God and the long-awaited Messiah of the Jews:

> The next day he saw Jesus coming to him, and said, "Behold, the Lamb of God who takes away the sin of the world! This is He in behalf of whom I said, 'After me is coming a Man who has proved to be my superior, because He existed before me.' And I did not recognize Him, but so that He would be revealed to Israel, I came baptizing in water." And John testified, saying, "I have seen the Spirit descending as a dove out of heaven, and He remained upon Him. And I did not recognize Him, but He who sent me to baptize in water said to me, 'He upon whom you see the Spirit descending and remaining upon Him, this is the One who baptizes in the Holy Spirit.' And I myself have seen, and have testified that this is the Son of God." Again the next day John was standing

with two of his disciples, and he looked at Jesus as He walked, and said, "Behold, the Lamb of God!" (John 1:29-36)

Most Jews would have also understood what John meant by calling Jesus, "the Lamb of God." Jesus *was* the Lamb of God, the Messiah, the Anointed One sent to be slain for the sins of the world.

But not in their wildest imaginations, or fears, could they conceive that their *fellow Jews* would be the ones doing the slaying.

Ultimately, though, Jews were not responsible for killing Jesus. No! It was the Father's plan all along to send His innocent Son—the Lamb of God—to be a blood sacrifice for the redemption of the *real* sinners: you and me. God foreshadowed this sacrifice in the beginning with Adam and Eve by *covering* the sins of the guilty with the shed blood of innocent animals:

And the Lord God made garments of skin for Adam and his wife, and clothed them. (Genesis 3:21)

This was after they tried to hide from God and cover their own sin with fig leaves. We can't cover our own sins, and only blood can atone for sin:

Then the eyes of both of them were opened, and they knew that they were naked; and they sewed fig leaves together and made themselves waist coverings. (Genesis 3:7)

Anointed as High Priest

Jesus also needed to fulfill the Old Testament priesthood law where priests were required to cleanse themselves before entering the tabernacle or temple. Jesus didn't have John baptize Him because God commanded it, since He was not of the line of Levi. But religious Jews would have expected it. They would never have accepted Jesus (most didn't anyway) without Him fulfilling that cleansing ritual. God had commanded Moses to have the Levitical priests, beginning with Aaron, cleanse themselves before entering His presence in the tabernacle, so Jesus had John baptize Him in the same manner:

> Then you shall bring Aaron and his sons to the doorway of the tent of meeting and wash them with water. (Exodus 29:4)

> Then the Lord spoke to Moses, saying, "You shall also make a basin of bronze, with its base of bronze, for washing; and you shall put it between the tent of meeting and the altar, and you shall put water in it. Aaron and his sons shall wash their hands and their feet from it; when they enter the tent of meeting, they shall wash with water, so that they do not die; or when they approach the altar to minister, by offering up in smoke a fire sacrifice to the Lord. So they shall wash their hands and their feet, so that they do not die; and it shall be a permanent statute for them, for Aaron and his descendants throughout their generations." (Exodus 30:17-21)

Jesus was from the line of Judah, not Levi. As the book of Hebrews reveals, though, Jesus was still a priest—High Priest—but in the order of Melchizedek:

> And no one can become a high priest simply because he wants such an honor. He must be called by God for this work, just as Aaron was. That is why Christ did not honor himself by assuming he could become High Priest. No, he was chosen by God, who said to him, "You are my Son. Today I have become your Father." And in another passage God said to him, "You are a priest forever in the order of Melchizedek." (Hebrews 5:4-6 NLT)

And further:

> In this way, God qualified him as a perfect High Priest, and he became the source of eternal salvation for all those who obey him. And God designated him to be a High Priest in the order of Melchizedek. (Hebrews 5:9-10 NLT)

No one would question if Jesus was a High Priest in the order of Levi, or Aaron, or even Moses. These are known, identifiable men of scripture. But who in the wide, wide world of mystery is this Melchizedek dude? And why would God use an "unknown" to substantiate His Son as High Priest?

The book of Hebrews gives us the amazing answers. Here is just some of what the writer shares to substantiate Melchizedek:

> There is no record of his father or mother or any of his ancestors—no beginning or end to his life. He remains a priest forever, resembling the Son of God.... Jesus became a priest, not by meeting the physical requirement of belonging to the tribe of Levi, but by the power of a life that cannot be destroyed.... Yes, the old requirement about the priesthood was set aside because it was weak and useless. For the law never made anything perfect. But now we have confidence in a better hope, through which we draw near to God.... Unlike those other high priests, he does not need to offer sacrifices every day. They did this for their own sins first and then for the sins of the people. But Jesus did this once for all when he offered himself as the sacrifice for the people's sins. (Hebrews 7:3, 16, 18-19, 27 NLT)

Jesus wouldn't enter the physical temple, though, with His sacrifice, but a temple made without hands:

> For Christ did not enter into a holy place made with human hands, which was only a copy of the true one in heaven. He entered into heaven itself to appear now before God on our behalf. (Hebrews 9:24 NLT)

Melchizedek appears in just one story of scripture, and there in only a few verses. He then departs just as quickly as he appeared. But God used him and his titles to substantiate Jesus as High Priest *and* King for His people:

> And Melchizedek, the king of Salem and a priest of God Most High, brought Abram some bread and wine. Melchizedek blessed Abram with this blessing: "Blessed be Abram by God Most High, Creator of heaven and earth. And blessed be God Most High, who has defeated your enemies for you." Then Abram gave Melchizedek a tenth of all the goods he had recovered. (Genesis 14:18-20 NLT)

A few decades after this encounter, God would designate Abraham's great-grandson, Levi (one of the twelve sons of Jacob), to serve Him by taking on full responsibility for the tabernacle (and later the temple). God would then call Levi's own great-grandson, Aaron (brother of Moses), to be the first Levite priest of the nation of Israel and lead the holy priests from that point forward.

Once each year, a priest would be selected as the high priest. He would enter the Most Holy Place on Yom Kippur (the Day of Atonement) to apply the blood of the sacrifice on the ark of the covenant. When Jesus said, "It is finished" while hanging on the cross, He was most specifically talking about this annual atonement—it was finished. It no longer needed to be made. Christ finished it with His death on the cross. The Israelites no longer needed to perform this annual ritual because He was their *final* sacrificial lamb.

In AD 70, though, God had to use the Roman army to destroy the holy temple in Jerusalem. This ended all temple sacrifices. The Israelites had not understood what Jesus accomplished by dying on the cross. They crucified Him because they had wanted Him to be their earthly king and destroy the Roman occupation of their land. Instead, God had the Roman army destroy their holy temple and city. They have not had a temple since that time and have not sacrificed any animals since. They still do not see that God destroyed the temple because it was no longer needed—He already sacrificed the last spotless Lamb for them.

This is why Jesus needed to be anointed as High Priest of God Most High—to become the *final* atoning blood sacrifice for the Jewish people. He did this by entering the Most Holy Place—heaven—once and for all time.

However, He was not High Priest in the order of Levi and Aaron but in the order of Melchizedek. Still, a priest nonetheless, so He needed to be "washed" (baptized) as God had commanded be done for holy priests.

(Jesus is also called "King of the Jews," which further identifies Him with Melchizedek, who was both priest *and* king.)

Other than a reference in Psalm 110:4, there is no other mention of Melchizedek in the Old Testament. No other stories, exploits, or even genealogy. He is referenced a few times in the New Testament, but only in Hebrews, a book written specifically to Jews.

Like Jesus Himself, the order of Melchizedek existed without God establishing it, hinting that it had always existed and would always exist. The priesthoods of Levi and Aaron, though, were established on earth, and they had a beginning and an ending.

Jesus was water-baptized for different reasons than believers today. Believers today get water-baptized to publicly proclaim their new life in Christ and that He is now Lord of their life.

Instead, Christ's water baptism fulfilled what God required:

- *Identified Him as a sinner so He could become the atoning sacrifice for the world*
- *Revealed Him as God's own Son, the Chosen One, the Messiah*
- *Rightfully anointed Him as High Priest*

Here is an amazing verse that connects all three of these reasons Jesus needed to be baptized in water:

> Therefore, it was necessary for him to be made in every respect like us, his brothers and sisters, so that he could be our merciful and faithful High Priest before God. Then he could offer a sacrifice that would take away the sins of the people. (Hebrews 2:17 NLT)

2) Spirit Baptism
Immediately after His water baptism, Jesus was baptized (immersed) with the Holy Spirit by His Father from heaven:

> After He was baptized, Jesus came up immediately from the water; and behold, the heavens were opened, and he [John] saw the Spirit of God descending as a dove and settling on Him, and behold, a voice from the heavens said, "This is My beloved Son, with whom I am well pleased." (Matthew 3:16-17)

While Jesus was and is God from before the events of Genesis 1:1 and was even the creator of all things (John 1:3), there are no scriptures that state He had the power of the Holy

Spirit upon Him prior to His Spirit baptism. That especially includes the power to perform miracles.

Indwelling versus Empowering

Being *indwelled* with the Holy Spirit is not the same as having the Holy Spirit *come upon* us in power. There is a clear biblical distinction between having the *indwelling* of the Holy Spirit and having the Holy Spirit *come upon* a believer with power.

This means two different biblical baptisms regarding the Holy Spirit. One where we are baptized *by the Holy Spirit* into the Body of Christ and receive the Holy Spirit to dwell in us, and a separate baptism where we are baptized *into the Holy Spirit* by Jesus for witnessing and for power:

> For by one Spirit we were all baptized into one body, whether Jews or Greeks, whether slaves or free, and we were all made to drink of one Spirit. (1 Corinthians 12:13)

> But you will receive power when the Holy Spirit has come upon you; and you shall be My witnesses both in Jerusalem and in all Judea, and Samaria, and as far as the remotest part of the earth. (Acts 1:8)

But if Jesus received the power of the Holy Spirit with His Spirit baptism, when did He receive the indwelling of the Holy Spirit?

While still in His mother's womb (I believe right at conception).

Scripture does not explicitly tell us this, but understanding two key points will leave little doubt.

First, Luke records what an angel of the Lord said to John the Baptist's father, Zechariah, when prophesying John's birth:

> For he will be great in the sight of the Lord; and he will drink no wine or liquor, and he will be filled with the Holy Spirit while still in his mother's womb. (Luke 1:15)

Second, God the Father in heaven *was* the Father of Jesus *through* the Holy Spirit:

> Now the birth of Jesus the Messiah was as follows: when His mother Mary had been betrothed to Joseph, before they came together she was found to be pregnant by the Holy Spirit. (Matthew 1:18)

And here, the angel Gabriel explained to Mary how she would conceive even though she was yet a virgin:

> But Mary said to the angel, "How will this be, since I am a virgin?" The angel answered and said to her, "The Holy Spirit will come upon you, and the power of the Most High will overshadow you; for that reason also the holy Child will be called the Son of God. (Luke 1:34-35)

So, if John the Baptist had the Holy Spirit dwelling in him while still in his mother's womb and the Holy Spirit conceived Jesus with God the Father as the father, it would be difficult to believe that Jesus did not already have the Holy Spirit in Him, at least at His birth if not at conception.

If Jesus had the indwelling of the Holy Spirit by His birth, His Spirit baptism at age thirty would have been a fully separate experience for a different purpose! He already had the Holy Spirit dwelling in Him, so He wouldn't need a second indwelling, but He would need the power of His Father for ministering.

Here's another way to look at this: If John the Baptist had the Holy Spirit in him from before birth, why didn't he perform miracles? Jesus also had the Holy Spirit, but, according to scripture, He only began performing miracles after He was baptized *with* the Holy Spirit by His Father while still in the Jordan River. The indwelling of the Holy Spirit doesn't bring God's power. That requires a separate event—the baptism with the Holy Spirit.

After His water and Spirit baptisms, Jesus was next led *by the Spirit* into the wilderness to be tempted by the devil. That's interesting timing, don't you think? Jesus would have needed the power of the Holy Spirit to survive those forty days of temptation without food and surrounded by wild beasts (Matthew 4:1-11; Mark 1:12-13; Luke 4:1-13).

So, not only did Jesus have a separate baptism with the Holy Spirit that brought power for ministry (as we'll see in the next two chapters), but His disciples did as well—and so can you and any believer in Jesus Christ.

Power for Ministry

But wait: If Jesus is God, why would He need to have the power of the Holy Spirit come upon Him? Wouldn't He already have all the power He needed at His birth?

We could ask the same question about wisdom: Wouldn't Jesus have known everything from His birth?

The answer to both questions is no.

We learn from Luke's gospel that Jesus's parents did not understand who He was, at least not at age twelve:

> And He said to them, "Why is it that you were looking for Me? Did you not know that I had to be in My Father's house?" And yet they on their part did not understand the statement which He had made to them. And He went down with them and came to Nazareth, and He continued to be subject to them; and His mother treasured all these things in her heart. (Luke 2:49-51)

If their son had been performing miracles during the first twelve years of His life, I doubt they would have misunderstood His statement or even been worried about Him. They would have already experienced Him performing miracles, talking about His Father's business, and going missing and returning without a worry.

And in the very next verse, we see Christ's humanity shown:

> And Jesus kept increasing in wisdom and stature, and in favor with God and people. (Luke 1:52)

Why would Jesus need to grow in wisdom if He was already God?

Because He was also man and needed to grow as a man in all ways so He could experience life as a human, understand our nature and frailty, and take our place on the cross.

There is no biblical evidence that Jesus had the power to perform miracles prior to His first public miracle of turning water into wine at the wedding of Cana (John 2:1-11). After all, Jewish people everywhere, including Christ's disciples, would certainly have heard about a miracle-working boy from Nazareth long before He began His ministry at age thirty, especially if He had been performing miracles in Nazareth while growing up. When He returned to His hometown, they would have readily welcomed Him back and celebrated Him as a hometown hero. Instead, they raged at Him and wanted to throw Him off a cliff! They just could not believe that this man who had recently been working miracles in nearby Capernaum and now claiming to be the Messiah was that same son of Joseph the carpenter:

> And all the people were speaking well of Him, and admiring the gracious words which were coming from His lips; and yet they were saying, "Is this not Joseph's son?" And He said to them, "No doubt you will quote this proverb to Me: 'Physician, heal yourself! All the miracles that we heard were done in Capernaum, do here in your hometown as well.'" But He said, "Truly I say to you, no prophet is welcome in his hometown."... And all the people in the synagogue were filled with rage as they heard these things; and they got up and drove Him out of the city, and brought Him to the crest of the hill on which their city had

been built, so that they could throw Him down from the cliff. But He passed through their midst and went on His way. (Luke 4:22-24, 28-30)

There is good indication, however, that Jesus *did* perform miracles *privately* prior to Cana, but certainly not before His Spirit baptism. As proof, consider these words of Mary at the wedding celebration in Cana:

> His mother said to the servants, "Whatever He tells you, do it." (John 2:5)

To explain this reasoning more clearly, here is the order of events in Jesus's first days of ministry:

- Water-baptized and Spirit-baptized (with power from on high)
- Led by the Spirit into the wilderness for forty days and tempted by the devil
- Private miracles (not recorded in scripture)
- First public miracle at Cana
- Other miracles (in Capernaum and other towns)
- Rejected in Nazareth, His hometown

Mary obviously had some experience with Jesus either performing miracles or producing top-rated wine without grapes. He was a carpenter, though, not a vintner.

For Mary to tell the servants to do whatever Jesus said to fix the wine problem indicates she knew He could do something special in moments like that. She also proved she was still "the mom" because she ignored His desire to not get involved:

> When the wine ran out, the mother of Jesus said to Him, "They have no wine." And Jesus said to her, "What business do you have with Me, woman? My hour has not yet come." (John 2:3-4)

I do not believe Jesus grew up performing miracles. There is nothing in scripture that supports this idea or even hints at it—including in the Old Testament, where we learn so much about the coming Messiah, but nothing about miracle-working powers until after His Spirit baptism.

Something happened between the ages of twelve and thirty that gave Jesus the power to perform miracles. That "something" was God the Father baptizing Him with the Holy Spirit immediately after John baptized Him with water in the Jordan River—right before the Spirit led Him into the wilderness for forty days.

It's not difficult to recognize that when the Holy Spirit falls on someone, they receive power. It happened to Jesus, to the disciples at Pentecost, and to other believers throughout the book of Acts, and it has continued to happen for the last two thousand years. No individual or incident in scripture illustrates this better than Jesus Himself with His clear and distinct baptism with the Holy Spirit in the Jordan River.

With Jesus's water baptism (anointing as High Priest) and Spirit baptism completed, He could now begin His earthly ministry. John the Baptist briefly continued his mission of preparing more hearts of the Jewish people for their Messiah but soon was beheaded by King Herod.

3) Cross (Grave) Baptism

Jesus told His disciples:

> I have come to cast fire upon the earth; and how I wish it were already kindled! But I have a baptism to undergo, and how distressed I am until it is accomplished! (Luke 12:49-50)

These verses reveal Christ's humanity. He wanted it over—not just His beatings and stripes and death and burial, but the coming tribulation as well. He wanted to get past these painful events and get on with His millennial reign and then on to the new heaven and new earth.

Casting fire upon the earth specifically refers to the time when He will unleash His wrath on the earth and bring an end to sin and death once and for all. His anguish isn't just for Himself but also for those who love Him and what they'll go through until He returns at His second coming.

We all have experienced moments in life when we must face the truth, face the pain of something, whether we brought it on ourselves or whether it was thrust on us. Jesus knows exactly how we feel. We want to skip it, get past the painful parts of life, and get on with the good stuff. Jesus was no different. He was God, but He was also human. He wanted to skip the pain but knew it was His Father's plan. This was His prayer to the Father that agonizing night in Gethsemane:

> And He went a little beyond them, and fell on His face and prayed, saying, "My Father, if it is possible, let this cup pass from Me; yet not as I will, but as You will." (Matthew 26:39)

The cup was His to carry and drink from. Abraham faced the same situation when God directed him to sacrifice his own firstborn son, Isaac, on an altar (Genesis 22:1-19). Abraham, most faithful Abraham, followed through because he trusted God. He knew that if Isaac died, God would resurrect him. *That is faith!*

But the angel of the Lord stopped him. God provided a ram instead for the sacrifice. Abraham called that place Jehovah Jireh—"the Lord will provide." In fact, God would later provide an even better sacrifice: *His* only begotten Son.

Bleeding not just drops of blood while praying in Gethsemane, Christ also bled the anxiety and anguish He carried. Alone in that garden, His humanity dripped out as well. He knew the pain He was about to face. He also knew He would endure it, but the whips would rip His flesh, the pain would be unbearably immense, and the emotional torment severe.

The *physical and emotional* pain that Jesus bore on our behalf was worse than any you or I will ever have to endure. It was this pain—these wounds—that freed us from our bondage to sin and made us right with God:

> But He was pierced for our offenses,
> He was crushed for our wrongdoings;
> The punishment for our well-being was laid upon Him,
> And by His wounds we are healed. (Isaiah 53:5)

Make no mistake: This was a baptism, an immersion into death. Christ Himself said it. However, it wasn't just an immersion into death and the grave, but into pain, anguish, and torment as well. Then came the nails. Through His hands and feet. Once nailed secure and hoisted high, He hung. In pain. The nails through His feet wrenched His bones as He tried to push Himself up. Relaxing, though, meant difficulty breathing. Then a spear tore into His side. Blood and water flowed. That brought a biting thirst. His eyes burning with blood and sweat, He caught a glimpse of his mother, Mary, as she watched in her own grief and pain. Then of John and the other disciples staring at Him. Wondering why He'd let this happen. Why He would disappoint them so. Among the chatter, He could hear the mockers, laughing at this fool on the cross. The light of the day darkened as death slipped in. He labored for His final breaths. The weight of the sins of the world magnified His pain.

Jesus's entire passion event was a baptism. He endured it all, though, for you and me.

Jesus didn't go to heaven upon His death. That wouldn't happen until His ascension forty-three days later. After His death, His body went into the tomb. His soul and spirit went to hades for three days and three nights. In Christ's own words:

> For just as Jonah was in the stomach of the sea monster for three days and three nights, so will the Son of Man be in the heart of the earth for three days and three nights. (Matthew 12:40)

Looking Back and Ahead

As you can see, scripture records very clearly and without question that Jesus experienced three baptisms:

1. Water: baptized in water by John the Baptist
2. Spirit: baptized with the Holy Spirit by His Father in heaven
3. Cross (grave): baptized into death by His Father

Let's carry our understanding of baptisms forward and next look at the three baptisms of His disciples.

6
The Three Baptisms of the Disciples

THE THREE BAPTISMS that the disciples experienced are not as clear in scripture as Christ's are, but we'll bring them to light in this chapter. Here are their three baptisms:

1. Water: They were baptized in water by John the Baptist or a fellow disciple.
2. Salvation: They were "born again" and baptized with (immersed with) the *indwelling* of the Holy Spirit by Jesus.
3. Spirit: They were baptized with the Holy Spirit by God/Jesus from heaven.

1) Water Baptism
Scripture records very clearly and without question that the disciples of Jesus experienced exactly... two baptisms. Yep, that's right. Just two are clearly recorded in scripture.

The missing baptism is their water baptism. However, no one questions whether the twelve disciples were in fact water-baptized or not. We can very confidently state that all twelve of the disciples were baptized in water, as were tens of thousands of other followers of Jesus during His earthly ministry.

Here are the two primary reasons for this confidence:

1. God sent John the Baptist to prepare the way for the Messiah. That was his sole assignment. When Jesus began His ministry, some of John's followers left him to join Jesus. (John was okay with this!) Andrew, Peter's brother, was one of those disciples, as shown in John 1:35-40. (A second disciple is mentioned but not named.) John certainly would have baptized his own disciples, or else he would not have allowed them to join his crew. John's ministry was to prepare the way for the Messiah, which meant calling for Jews to repent and be baptized in water. Andrew and the other disciples who left John's ministry to join Jesus would have carried that ministry of water baptism forward with them.
2. Jesus's ministry included water baptisms as well. He, too, would have required His disciples to repent and be baptized because they would be the ones performing the baptisms, not Himself:

> So then, when the Lord knew that the Pharisees had heard that He was making and baptizing more disciples than John (although Jesus Himself was not baptizing; rather, His disciples were), He left Judea and went away again to Galilee. (John 4:1-3)

Don't think for a second that Jesus and John were competing to see who could build the bigger ministry (i.e., have the larger congregation). That was not God's calling on either of their lives. John was preparing the way for Jesus to be the Messiah for the Jews, and he fully understood that his ministry would diminish so Jesus's could grow. John was blunt about his calling when his own disciples told him everyone was bypassing him and instead going to Jesus:

> You yourselves are my witnesses that I said, "I am not the Christ," but, "I have been sent ahead of Him." He who has the bride is the groom; but the friend of the groom, who stands and listens to him, rejoices greatly because of the groom's voice. So this joy of mine has been made full. He must increase, but I must decrease. (John 3:28-30)

The water baptisms of the disciples are not recorded in scripture, because, in my opinion, they just weren't important to the narrative. Jesus's water baptism was an important event, but not theirs. Every detail in the Bible is there for a reason. Any details left out were left out for a reason, including lack of importance. The water baptisms of the disciples just didn't move God's redemption story along—Jesus's certainly did, though.

We can confidently say that the disciples of Jesus were baptized in water. There is no indication that they weren't, only strong indication that they were.

2) Salvation Baptism

Okay, we're about to step in it—a big muddy mess. We're going from nonexistent scripture but certainty of water baptisms for the disciples to actual scripture showing their salvation baptism, though layered in the muck of complexity and confusion.

Before we begin this discussion, though, we need to step back and present a scriptural foundation regarding salvations. These biblical facts will significantly improve your comprehension of how the disciples were saved. Without this understanding, we'd be left puzzled and guessing at what really happened in John 20:22 and subsequently at the Day of Pentecost in Acts 2.

As you read this section, keep in mind that we are talking about the days of Jesus's earthly ministry all the way through the day of His resurrection. These events all occurred under the Old Testament covenant of law *specific to Jews*. None of this was for Gentiles, and none of it includes salvation by grace or by the cross or by the blood of Jesus. Salvation in the days of Jesus and the disciples was different than how we are saved today, as we examined earlier.

I realize this sounds like heresy, but I promise you, it's not. If you desire the truth of scripture, read on. If you prefer to believe only what you've been told, then toss this book.

No One Is in Hell Because of Their Sins

The Bible is so simple yet so complex. From Genesis through Revelation, it is simply the story of God's love for all humankind and His desire to redeem us—to purchase us back from the grip of sin and death we put ourselves into. At the same time, the complexity ebbs and flows throughout the seven thousand years of details from Genesis through Revelation.

In the beginning, we were destined to live with God forever in the Garden of Eden as His perfect, sinless creation—His children created in His image. But rather than program us to love Him as if we were robots, He instead gave us a free will. That free will gives each of us the ability to make choices. Good choices. And bad ones.

Now, Satan lusted after all of humankind and the earth. He wanted it all for his own selfish, evil purposes. So, he deceived Eve. Adam made the situation eternally worse by exercising his free will to deliberately sin against God. And just like that, the whole human race fell. Everyone unwittingly tumbled forward through the centuries like millions and millions of dominoes toppling forward onto each other because of the sin of those who fell before them.

The immediate death that Adam and Eve experienced, though, was spiritual, not physical. It also brought them, and us, eternal separation from God. Since those bites of fruit, no one has been able to hide their sin or themselves from God. We all foolishly work to "perfect" our way back to God, but that always proves a miserable failure.

We are powerless to save ourselves.

Adam's original sin also introduced *physical death* into our destiny. We cannot escape this death either.

But wait! It gets worse.

We are all destined to die a *second death* as well. This second death—a spiritual death—will occur at the great white throne of judgment at the end of Christ's millennial reign. This judgment brings final *eternal* separation from God:

> The one who has an ear, let him hear what the Spirit says to the churches. The one who overcomes will not be hurt by the second death. (Revelation 2:11)

> But for the cowardly, and unbelieving, and abominable, and murderers, and sexually immoral persons, and sorcerers, and idolaters, and all liars, their part will be in the lake that burns with fire and brimstone, which is the second death. (Revelation 21:8)

Yikes!

But God sent us His Good News.

He sent His Son, Jesus, to shed His blood for us on Calvary. As a result, we can all experience becoming a new creation in Christ. We can be made clean as if we've never sinned, and *never* experience that second death.

Let me put it even more simply:

No one has ever been sent to hell because of the sins they committed. Not one person. Ever.

God doesn't send people to hell because of their sins—no matter how horrible their sins might be.

In fact, God doesn't send *anyone* to hell. He never has.

That's not who He is. It's not the job He assigned Himself. It's not even His decision. It's our decision.

We choose to spend eternity in hell.

How?

By making one small decision: rejecting God's only Son and the blood He shed for us on the cross.

That's it.

That's the only thing that has ever or will ever send anyone to hell.

We make the choice to spend eternity in hell simply because we reject His offer of redemption—total forgiveness and complete covering of our sins by the blood of His Son.

To be saved, delivered from our destiny of eternity in the lake of fire, we only need to believe in what Jesus did for us—that He died for us on the cross, was buried in the grave, and rose again three days later.

That's it. That's the gospel that saves today. Jesus revealed it to the apostle Paul, and Paul included it in a letter to the Corinthian church:

> Let me now remind you, dear brothers and sisters, of the Good News I preached to you before. You welcomed it then, and you still stand firm in it. It is this Good News that saves you if you continue to believe the message I told you—unless, of course, you believed something that was never true in the first place. I passed on to you what was most important and what had also been passed on to me. Christ died for our sins, just as the Scriptures said. He was buried, and he was raised from the dead on the third day, just as the Scriptures said. (1 Corinthians 15:1-4 NLT)

Everyone makes this decision on their own. We either believe in what Jesus did for us on the cross or we don't. We either believe Him or we don't. We either accept Him or reject Him.

For those of us who *do believe* that Jesus shed His blood on the cross for our sins, was then buried, and rose again three days later, *we will not* face a second death. That's God's promise to us. To anyone who believes.

Instead, we will spend the remainder of eternity with Him and His Son in heaven. We won't see or feel even a lick of those scorching hot flames.

That's a promise that God nailed to the cross two thousand years ago for you and for me:

> Then, together with them, we who are still alive and remain on the earth will be caught up in the clouds to meet the Lord in the air. Then we will be with the Lord forever. (1 Thessalonians 4:17 NLT)

A New Covenant

So, Adam sinned, and we fell.

God then kicked Adam and Eve out of Eden, and we've all been born into separation from Him ever since.

He has given us the opportunity to be in relationship with Him once again, though. The first opportunity was to the Israelite nation through the promises and covenants He made with their forefathers—Abraham and Moses. When the Israelites, as the Jewish people, eventually rejected Jesus (crucified Him), God opened salvation up to *anyone* who would believe that His Son died to pay the price for their sins.

He is inviting all to come and be in right standing with Him once again through the redeeming blood of His Son.

Instead of eternal damnation in the lake of fire, believers receive everlasting life with Him in heaven. We also receive the peace of Christ because we are back in relationship with God our Father.

That should have been you nailed to that cross. It should have been me. And it should still be. Jesus took our place, though. He didn't have to. God did not force Him onto that cross (Philippians 2:6-8). He *chose* to obey His Father so that you and I might live—abundantly, spiritually, eternally. We not only receive abundant life and freedom now but also everlasting life after we die.

Jesus became our righteousness so we could one day stand before God righteous and sinless. Our perfect, sinless Savior has covered our multitude of sins, and the Father invites us to join Him once again in Eden—this time forever.

The Bible is overwhelmingly a Jewish (Hebrew) book. By *Jewish*, I don't just mean solely from the line of Jacob (Israel) or Judah, but the line of Abraham-Isaac-Jacob. We Gentiles tend to view all forerunners to Abraham as Jewish as well, even though technically they weren't. They were chosen by God, though, so in that sense, they are still God's chosen people.

The Bible was written mostly *by* Jews (except the gospel of Luke and book of Acts) and *to* Jews. The apostle Paul's writings, however, are written to believers, those baptized into the Body of Christ. In the Body of Christ, there are no Jews or Gentiles, only those "in Christ" (Galatians 3:28).

All prophecy in the Old Testament was for Jews. However, the apostle Paul tells us that we Gentiles have been grafted in:

> But some of these branches from Abraham's tree—some of the people of Israel—have been broken off. And you Gentiles, who were branches from a wild olive tree, have been grafted in. So now you also receive the blessing God has promised Abraham and his children, sharing in the rich nourishment from the root of God's special olive tree. (Romans 11:17 NLT)

As you can see, the promises God made to Abraham were solely between Him and His chosen nation, Israel. This is especially true of the covenants He made with Abraham directly. But He didn't forget about the rest of us. Gentiles are grafted into His promises—we get to benefit too! Israel first, though, then Gentiles.

There is no covenant more important in this church age (age of grace) than the new covenant, which Jeremiah prophesied about:

> "Behold, days are coming," declares the Lord, "when I will make a new covenant with the house of Israel and the house of Judah, not like the covenant which I made with their fathers on the day I took them by the hand to bring them out of the land of Egypt, My covenant which they broke, although I was a husband to them," declares the Lord. "For this is the covenant which I will make with the house of Israel after those days," declares the Lord: "I will put My law within them and write it on their heart; and I will be their God, and they shall be My people. They will not teach again, each one his neighbor and each one his brother, saying, 'Know the Lord,' for they will all know Me, from the least of them

to the greatest of them," declares the Lord, "for I will forgive their wrongdoing, and their sin I will no longer remember." (Jeremiah 31:31-34)

In this new covenant, God puts His law within us; He writes it on our hearts. This is not the law once written on stone (that is, the Ten Commandments), but a new law now written on our hearts with the blood of His Son. Those who choose to believe are free from the penalty of sin that the original law made abundantly evident.

Unfortunately, Jews who do not accept Christ as their Savior forfeit the promises of the new covenant that God originally gave to them. They rejected their Messiah (as a nation) and must now wait until the tribulation to even understand it, and then wait for the millennial kingdom to finally live it out. That is when Jesus will finally be their King, which they expected Him to be at His first coming.

This new covenant was originally, and is still, between God and His people Israel. But God calls for Gentiles ("the nations") to also be blessed through Abraham as well.

This new covenant began at Christ's death and is still in force today. However, it will not be fully completed until the millennial kingdom arrives at Christ's second coming.

In the Old Testament, God made it clear that He desires redemption for all people—Jews and Gentiles alike—by charging Jeremiah to be a prophet to non-Jews as well (again, "the nations"):

> Before I formed you in the womb I knew you,
> And before you were born I consecrated you;

> I have appointed you as a prophet to the nations.
> (Jeremiah 1:5)

Then, in the New Testament, Paul tells us that God always intended to include Gentiles in His plan of salvation and blessings, but held it back as a *mystery* until after Christ's death, revealing it *only* to the apostle Paul:

> As I briefly wrote earlier, God himself revealed his mysterious plan to me. As you read what I have written, you will understand my insight into this plan regarding Christ. God did not reveal it to previous generations, but now by his Spirit he has revealed it to his holy apostles and prophets. And this is God's plan: Both Gentiles and Jews who believe the Good News share equally in the riches inherited by God's children. Both are part of the same body, and both enjoy the promise of blessings because they belong to Christ Jesus. (Ephesians 3:3-6 NLT)

> As He also says in Hosea: "I will call those who were not My people, 'My people,' and her who was not beloved, 'beloved.' And it shall be that in the place where it was said to them, 'You are not My people,' there they shall be called sons of the living God." (Romans 9:25-26)

Paul also confirms for us who the real children of Abraham are:

> In the same way, "Abraham believed God, and God counted him as righteous because of his faith." The real children of Abraham, then, are those who put their faith in God. What's more, the Scriptures looked forward to this time when God would make the Gentiles right in his sight because of their faith. God proclaimed this good news to Abraham long ago when he said, "All nations will be blessed through you." So all who put their faith in Christ share the same blessing Abraham received because of his faith. (Galatians 3:6-9 NLT)

We even see a hint of God including Gentiles in His plans way back in Genesis when He first spoke to Abraham (as Abram):

> I will bless those who bless you and curse those who treat you with contempt. All the families on earth will be blessed through you. (Genesis 12:3 NLT)

Finally, during the Last Supper, Jesus declared that the new covenant *was by His blood* and commanded us to remember it until He returns (Matthew 26:26-29; Mark 14:22-25; Luke 22:14-20).

In his first letter to the Corinthian church, Paul emphasized the importance of both Christ's new covenant and the communion we take to remember it:

> For I received from the Lord that which I also delivered to you, that the Lord Jesus, on the night when He was betrayed, took bread; and when He had given thanks, He broke it and said, "This is My body, which is for you; do this in remembrance of Me." In the same way He also took the cup after supper, saying, "This cup is the new covenant in My blood; do this, as often as you drink it, in remembrance of Me." For as often as you eat this bread and drink the cup, you proclaim the Lord's death until He comes. (1 Corinthians 11:23-26)

A New Gospel

All Christians need to clearly understand that the gospel that saves today was *not* the gospel Jesus preached. It also was *not* the gospel by which the disciples were saved. It can't be. Read on, but please don't just take my word for it; search and study the scriptures for yourself!

We are saved today by the grace of God who chose to send His Son to shed His blood for our sins. He left heaven, left His Father, to come to earth. He became human so that He could understand the trials and joys of this life. He came to take our place on the cross, just as He took the place of Barabbas, the thief, on the middle cross.

But while He was on earth, Jesus did not preach His blood as an atoning sacrifice for our sins. He also never preached the cross. He couldn't preach these because He hadn't yet died. He wouldn't shed His blood for anyone until the very end of His earthly ministry.

John's gospel gives us the closest Jesus came in His ministry to proclaiming the gospel that saves today—salvation by way of our sins being nailed with Him to the cross, our sins forever covered by His blood—during His conversation with Nicodemus about the need to be "born again":

> And just as Moses lifted up the serpent in the wilderness, so must the Son of Man be lifted up, so that everyone who believes will have eternal life in Him. (John 3:14-15)

Here, Jesus was referencing a time in the wilderness when the Israelites grumbled against God and Moses (Numbers 21:4-9). As a result, God sent fiery serpents among them, and many died. Moses interceded for the people and God relented. He told Moses to make a bronze serpent and lift it up onto a pole. If anyone was bitten, they could look up at the bronze serpent and live.

This event foreshadowed Jesus being lifted up on the cross as our sin. But Jesus didn't explain to Nicodemus what He meant by this reference to Moses, nor did He explain anytime later in His ministry the connection between His blood, the cross, and forgiveness of sins. He just kept preaching the gospel of the kingdom of God to Jews, which was to believe that He was the Messiah, the Son of God, and to repent (change your mind about God), be water-baptized, and continue following the law.

Table 2 gives an overview of the difference between the two gospels of Jesus: the gospel of the kingdom and the gospel of grace.

In Romans 16, Paul calls the gospel of grace that he preaches "my gospel." As he explains, it was a mystery until Jesus revealed it to him, meaning the gospel of the kingdom that Jesus, Peter, and the other disciples preached had to be a different gospel since it was hidden by God until Paul was called on the road to Damascus. Jesus and His disciples preached only to Jews while Paul preached this new gospel to both Jews and Gentiles, though ultimately only to Gentiles:

> Now to Him who is able to establish you according to **my gospel** and the preaching of Jesus Christ, according to the revelation of the mystery which has been kept secret for long ages past, (Romans 16:25)

As you can see, the gospel that Jesus and His disciples preached during their ministry was much different than the gospel that saves today.

Here are a few verses showing the requirements for salvation during the ministries of Jesus, John the Baptist, and the disciples:

> John the Baptist appeared in the wilderness, preaching a baptism of repentance for the forgiveness of sins. And all the country of Judea was going out to him, and all the people of Jerusalem; and they were being baptized by him in the Jordan River, confessing their sins. (Mark 1:4-5)

The Two Gospels	
Gospel of the Kingdom of God	**Gospel of the Grace of God**
Proclaimed by Jesus, His disciples, John the Baptist	Proclaimed by Paul and his followers
Active during Jesus's earthly ministry and into the ministry of His apostles	Active from Acts 9 onward, including today
For Jews only	For all people, whether Jew or Gentile
Will be a physical kingdom on earth with Jesus as Israel's King (the millennial kingdom)	Will be in heaven with Jesus as Lord over all
Required faith + repentance + water baptism + works of the law	Requires faith + nothing else (Eph. 2:8-9)
Faith = belief in His name, Jesus as Messiah, the Son of God	Faith = belief in the death, burial, and resurrection of Jesus (1 Cor. 15:1-4)
Began with John the Baptist	Began with Jesus calling Paul (Acts 9)
Ended at or soon after the Council at Jerusalem (Acts 15)	Will end with the rapture of the Body of Christ

— Table 2 —

> Now after John was taken into custody, Jesus came into Galilee, preaching the gospel of God, and saying, "The time is fulfilled, and the kingdom of God is at hand; repent and believe in the gospel." (Mark 1:14-15)

> From that time Jesus began to preach and say, "Repent, for the kingdom of heaven is at hand." (Matthew 4:17)

> Jesus was going about in all of Galilee, teaching in their synagogues and proclaiming the gospel of the kingdom, and healing every disease and every sickness among the people. (Matthew 4:23)

> But as many as received Him, to them He gave the right to become children of God, to those who believe in His name. (John 1:12)

Even after Christ's ascension, Peter and his fellow disciples continued to preach the gospel of the kingdom—and to Israel only, as seen here when Peter preached on the Day of Pentecost, ten days after Jesus ascended to heaven:

> "Therefore let **all the house of Israel** know for certain that God has made Him both Lord and Christ—this Jesus whom you crucified." Now when they heard this, they were pierced to the heart, and said to Peter and the rest of the apostles, "Brothers, what are we to do?" Peter said to them, "Repent, and each of you be

baptized in the name of Jesus Christ for the forgiveness of your sins; and you will receive the gift of the Holy Spirit." (Acts 2:36-38)

These verses were directed solely to Jews. Gentiles did not believe in God at that time. Jesus and His disciples *never* took the Good News of the kingdom of God to Gentiles during His earthly ministry:

> These twelve Jesus sent out after instructing them, saying, "Do not go on a road to Gentiles, and do not enter a city of Samaritans; but rather go to the lost sheep of the house of Israel. And as you go, preach, saying, 'The kingdom of heaven has come near.'" (Matthew 10:5-7)

Jesus even told a Canaanite (Gentile) woman that He was sent to preach only to Jews:

> But He answered and said, "I was sent only to the lost sheep of the house of Israel." (Matthew 15:24)

Our salvation today is not secured by believing in His name, by repentance, by water baptism, or by following the law. We are saved by the gospel of grace, the gospel that Jesus revealed only to Paul. This gospel requires faith in His death, burial, and resurrection, as recorded in 1 Corinthians 15:1-4.

In addition to not preaching the cross or His blood, Jesus also did not preach that salvation was by grace through faith. He couldn't because He only revealed that mystery to the apostle Paul *after* Paul was converted—the mystery that Paul later explained to the church in Rome:

> For everyone has sinned; we all fall short of God's glorious standard. **Yet God, in his grace, freely makes us right in his sight.** He did this through Christ Jesus when he freed us from the penalty for our sins. For God presented Jesus as the sacrifice for sin. **People are made right with God when they believe that Jesus sacrificed his life, shedding his blood.** This sacrifice shows that God was being fair when he held back and did not punish those who sinned in times past. (Romans 3:23-25 NLT)

This was not how Jesus told Jews they would be made righteous, made right with God.

As well, Jesus also revealed other truths to Paul, which Paul in turn wrote about thirty years after Christ's death:

> For the grace of God has been revealed, bringing salvation to all people. (Titus 2:11 NLT)

> I want them to be encouraged and knit together by strong ties of love. I want them to have complete confidence that they understand God's mysterious plan, which is Christ himself. (Colossians 2:2 NLT)

Our confidence is in Christ Himself and what He did on the cross, not in who He was, or in repentance, or water baptism, or following the laws of Moses.

And finally…

> You were dead because of your sins and because your sinful nature was not yet cut away. Then God made you alive with Christ, for he forgave all our sins. He canceled the record of the charges against us and took it away by nailing it to the cross. (Colossians 2:13-14 NLT)

> For Christ didn't send me to baptize, but to preach the Good News—and not with clever speech, for fear that the cross of Christ would lose its power. The message of the cross is foolish to those who are headed for destruction! But we who are being saved know it is the very power of God. (1 Corinthians 1:17-18 NLT)

The disciples of Jesus, though truly honorable and world-changing men of God, did not understand the gospel by which we are saved today—the grace of God through faith in the death, burial, and resurrection of Jesus:

> Now He took the twelve aside and said to them, "Behold, we are going up to Jerusalem, and all the things that have been written through the prophets about the Son of Man will be accomplished. For He will be handed over to the Gentiles, and will be ridiculed, and abused, and spit upon, and after they have flogged Him, they will kill Him; and on the third day He will rise." **The disciples understood none of these things**, and the meaning of this statement was hidden from them, and they did not comprehend the things that were said. (Luke 18:31-34)

In Acts 15—eighteen years after Christ's death—Peter came close to proclaiming the gospel of grace. In Acts 15:11, while meeting with Paul, James, and other leading apostles at the Council at Jerusalem, Peter stated that Jews and Gentiles alike are "saved through the grace of the Lord Jesus."

This was very different than the message he preached on the Day of Pentecost in Acts 2! He did not preach grace to the Israelites that day, nor the cross, nor the blood.

But, in Acts 15, eighteen years later, he revealed his understanding of the grace of God, though still not mentioning the cross or the blood of Christ. Then, sixteen years after this meeting in Jerusalem (thirty-four years after Jesus's death), Peter wrote the following to believing Jews outside of Jerusalem:

> … knowing that you were not redeemed with perishable things like silver or gold from your futile way of life inherited from your forefathers, but with precious blood, as of a lamb unblemished and spotless, the blood of Christ. (1 Peter 1:18-19)

Thirty-four years after Jesus was crucified, Peter finally revealed that he understood the gospel that Jesus revealed to Paul, the gospel that saves today—a very different gospel than Jesus, the disciples, and John the Baptist had preached to Israel.

In his second letter to Jewish believers, though, Peter admitted something important—that he'd always had difficulty understanding Paul's gospel message. That was why it took so many years for him to understand the grace of God, and even longer to fully grasp the real purpose of Christ's shed blood on the cross. In the end, he finally agreed with Paul and even pointed to him as receiving wisdom from God:

> And remember, our Lord's patience gives people time to be saved. This is what our beloved brother Paul also wrote to you with the wisdom God gave him—speaking of these things in all of his letters. Some of his comments are hard to understand, and those who are ignorant and unstable have twisted his letters to mean something quite different, just as they do with other parts of Scripture. And this will result in their destruction. (2 Peter 3:15-16 NLT)

As I reflect on this, I was saved for *thirty-six years* before I fully understood and accepted the grace of God and the blood of my Savior shed on that cross on Calvary.

The apostle John wrote three epistles, and in them, he also touched on the new covenant gospel that Jesus revealed to Paul—but *sixty years* after Christ's death:

> But if we walk in the Light as He Himself is in the Light, we have fellowship with one another, and the blood of Jesus His Son cleanses us from all sin. (1 John 1:7)

> He himself is the sacrifice that atones for our sins—and not only our sins but the sins of all the world. (1 John 2:2 NLT)

So, some thirty-four years after Jesus's death, Peter finally proclaimed that the blood of Christ redeems us from sin and eternal destruction. Likewise, sixty years after Christ's death, the apostle John also showed he finally understood the true purpose of the cross, the blood, and the grace of God that brought salvation to all people.

Let's get back to our look at how the disciples were saved.

If Jesus never preached the gospel of salvation by grace through faith during His earthly ministry, and if the disciples did not fully understand it until thirty to sixty years later, then they *could not* have been saved by grace or the cross or the blood while Jesus was physically with them and certainly not before He was crucified!

These biblical truths are important to understand because they will help make sense of how the disciples were in fact saved and of the salvation baptism they experienced. Without this understanding, we would be left guessing at what really happened in John 20:22 on the day Christ resurrected and what happened fifty days later on the Day of Pentecost in Acts 2.

The Disciples Receive Their Salvation
The disciples were saved in two steps:

- First, they were each saved by the gospel of the kingdom. They individually repented, were water-baptized, continued to follow the law, and proclaimed their belief in Jesus as the Messiah, the Son of God.

- Second, their salvation was complete when they were "born again" by receiving the indwelling of the Holy Spirit from Jesus *after* He was resurrected (John 20:22).

Table 2 shows the disciples would have needed faith (belief) + repentance + water baptism + works of the law to be saved according to the gospel of the kingdom of God, which was God's program of salvation in the days of Jesus's ministry.

We just gave proof that they certainly had repented and were water-baptized by John the Baptist or a fellow disciple of his or a disciple of Jesus.

They were also certainly following the law, as Jesus Himself would have been and would have required of His disciples. The law wasn't just the Ten Commandments, though, but also 603 additional laws in the Torah. As we've already seen, even Jesus said that He didn't come to abolish the law and the prophets, but to fulfill them. But He would not fulfill them until His death on the cross.

That left just one "work" remaining for the disciples to be saved: proclaim their faith.

Jesus Himself would later take care of the final aspect: indwell them with the Holy Spirit.

So, did the disciples prove they in fact believed that Jesus was the Messiah, the Son of God?

Absolutely!

Now, scripture doesn't record every disciple verbalizing their faith, but it does show Jesus telling them that true faith is required. And He would not have given them the indwelling Spirit if they had not already proven or verbalized their faith in who He was.

Peter Confesses His Belief
Here, Peter proved to Jesus that he believed in Him as the Christ, the Messiah, the Son of God:

> Now when Jesus came into the region of Caesarea Philippi, He was asking His disciples, "Who do people say that the Son of Man is?" And they said, "Some say John the Baptist; and others, Elijah; and still others, Jeremiah, or one of the other prophets." He said to them, "But who do you yourselves say that I am?" Simon Peter answered, "You are the Christ, the Son of the living God." And Jesus said to him, "Blessed are you, Simon Barjona, because flesh and blood did not reveal this to you, but My Father who is in heaven." (Matthew 16:13-17)

Notice that Jesus told Peter that he didn't know this by his own flesh-and-blood knowledge, but that the Father in heaven revealed it to him. Today, it's the Holy Spirit that gives believers knowledge from God. But Peter did not yet have the Holy Spirit in him. If he did, Jesus would have told Peter that the Holy Spirit revealed this to him. Without the indwelling of the Holy Spirit, Peter clearly could not have been born again.

Remember also that Peter would soon reject Jesus on the night of His crucifixion. Three times he would deny knowing Him. Then, after Jesus's death and burial, the disciples were hiding in the upper room, afraid that the Jewish leaders would come after them next.

Peter was not yet fully saved or born again. His actions were not those of a saved, Holy Spirit-filled believer.

Thomas Believes

Jesus was resurrected on the first day of the week (Sunday). That same evening, the disciples were in the upper room when

Jesus appeared to them. One disciple was missing, though: Thomas. *After* Jesus left them, this was what happened:

> But Thomas, one of the twelve, who was called Didymus, was not with them when Jesus came. So the other disciples were saying to him, "We have seen the Lord!" But he said to them, "Unless I see in His hands the imprint of the nails, and put my finger into the place of the nails, and put my hand into His side, I will not believe." Eight days later His disciples were again inside, and Thomas was with them. Jesus came, the doors having been shut, and stood in their midst and said, "Peace be to you." Then He said to Thomas, "Place your finger here, and see My hands; and take your hand and put it into My side; and do not continue in disbelief, but be a believer." Thomas answered and said to Him, "My Lord and my God!" (John 20:24-28)

Thomas needed to see the resurrected Christ for himself to believe. He did not believe in who Jesus was prior to this moment. But Peter believed before he encountered the *resurrected* Christ. Regarding the other disciples, without definitive proof, we can only guess that they proclaimed belief that Jesus was the expected Messiah and the Son of God sometime throughout their three years with Him. Andrew, Philip, and Nathanael may have been the first to believe. (See John 1:43-51 for this story.) It appears certain, though, that Thomas may have been the laggard of the group.

The disciples were still missing a baptism, though, to fully complete their salvation. They had done their part—repented, received water baptism, followed the law, and proclaimed their belief in Jesus as the Messiah, the Son of God. But they had not yet received the indwelling of the Holy Spirit. Jesus revealed earlier in His ministry that they needed the Spirit to be "born again."

So, let's return to that story of Nicodemus, the Pharisee who asked Jesus how someone could be born again:

> Now there was a man of the Pharisees, named Nicodemus, a ruler of the Jews; this man came to Jesus at night and said to Him, "Rabbi, we know that You have come from God as a teacher; for no one can do these signs that You do unless God is with him." Jesus responded and said to him, **"Truly, truly, I say to you, unless someone is born again he cannot see the kingdom of God."** Nicodemus said to Him, "How can a person be born when he is old? He cannot enter his mother's womb a second time and be born, can he?" Jesus answered, **"Truly, truly, I say to you, unless someone is born of water and the Spirit, he cannot enter the kingdom of God.** That which has been born of the flesh is flesh, and that which has been born of the Spirit is spirit." (John 3:1-6)

Every human is born of water—that is, born of a mother, born of flesh. But not everyone is born of the Spirit. Receiving the Holy Spirit is required for being born again. This was exactly what happened to the disciples in John 20:22. This was the moment their faith + repentance + water baptism + works of the law met with the indwelling Holy Spirit and brought them new life in Jesus Christ—the moment they were born again:

> And when He had said this, He breathed on them and said to them, "Receive the Holy Spirit." (John 20:22)

Let's rewind time a few months and see how Jesus prophesied that the disciples would receive the indwelling of the Holy Spirit:

> I will ask the Father, and He will give you another Helper, so that He may be with you forever; the Helper is the Spirit of truth, **whom the world cannot receive**, because it does not see Him or know Him; but you know Him because He remains with you **and will be in you.** (John 14:16-17)

Notice that Jesus said the Holy Spirit was *with them* but would be *in them*. He also said that the world could not receive the Holy Spirit because they did "not see Him or know Him." This was where their faith + repentance + water baptism + works of the law proved to Jesus that they were not of the world but were of God and could rightly receive the indwelling Holy Spirit.

This is *not* how we are saved today! That was for Jews only during the ministry of Jesus, John the Baptist, and the disciples. Our salvation is solely by God's grace + our faith in the death, burial, and resurrection of Jesus Christ, + nothing else.

This indwelling baptism of the disciples occurred the evening Christ was resurrected, when Doubting Thomas was not with them. The disciples were in the upper room hiding from the Jewish religious leaders, wondering what they were going to do without Jesus:

> Now when it was evening on that day, the first day of the week, and when the doors were shut where the disciples were together due to fear of the Jews, Jesus came and stood in their midst, and said to them, "Peace be to you." And when He had said this, He showed them both His hands and His side. The disciples then rejoiced when they saw the Lord. So Jesus said to them again, "Peace be to you; just as the Father has sent Me, I also send you." And when He had said this, He breathed on them and said to them, "Receive the Holy Spirit." (John 20:19-22)

God is not going to leave us wondering, though, if this really was the moment the disciples were born again, when they were given "new life." He had already breathed out new life *twice* before in scripture! First, when He created Adam and later when He gave Ezekiel a prophetic vision to bring dead bodies to life in the Valley of Dry Bones:

> Then the Lord God formed the man of dust from the ground, and breathed into his nostrils the breath of life; and the man became a living person. (Genesis 2:7)

> So I prophesied as He commanded me, and the breath entered them, and they came to life and stood on their feet, an exceedingly great army. (Ezekiel 37:10)

The disciples were born again spiritually when God breathed life into them by way of Jesus in John 20—exactly like Adam when he was newly born. They were truly given new life when they received the Holy "Breath" of God, the Holy Spirit. You and I have also received into us *this same* Holy Breath—the same Holy Spirit of the living God—in the moment of our own salvation.

God giving the Holy Spirit is an essential part of the new covenant in Jesus that we covered earlier:

> Then I will sprinkle clean water on you, and you will be clean; I will cleanse you from all your filthiness and from all your idols. Moreover, I will give you a new heart and put a new spirit within you; and I will remove the heart of stone from your flesh and give you a heart of flesh. And I will put My Spirit within you and bring it about that you walk in My statutes, and are careful and follow My ordinances. (Ezekiel 36:25-27)

This baptism brings an immersion of the *indwelling* Holy Spirit. This is a totally separate Holy Spirit baptism from what the disciples would experience next, on the Day of Pentecost. That was when they would be baptized *with the Holy Spirit and power*. These are scripturally separate and distinct baptisms for the disciples.

You and I can also experience these two separate and distinct baptisms—one at our salvation when we receive the indwelling of the Holy Spirit and one at our Spirit baptism when He comes upon us with power. We get to breathe in *the exact same Spirit* that was in Jesus and that He breathed into His disciples that brought them new life:

> For by one Spirit we were all baptized into one body, whether Jews or Greeks, whether slaves or free, and we were all made to drink of one Spirit. (1 Corinthians 12:13)

Same God. Same breath. Same Holy Spirit. Same effect. How beautiful is that? God is so awesome!

Let's move on to the third and final baptism of the disciples: baptism in the Holy Spirit.

3) *Holy Spirit Baptism*

Jesus not only breathed the Holy Spirit into the disciples, but He also promised them if He returned to heaven, His Father would send the gift of the Holy Spirit. Before Jesus made His promise, though, both Joel and John the Baptist prophesied this outpouring. Here is what Joel wrote some 860 years earlier:

> It will come about after this
> That I will pour out My Spirit on all mankind;
> And your sons and your daughters will prophesy,
> Your old men will have dreams,
> Your young men will see visions.
> And even on the male and female servants
> I will pour out My Spirit in those days. (Joel 2:28-29)

We know that Joel prophesied this about the Holy Spirit coming on the Day of Pentecost in AD 30 because Peter repeated the prophecy in his sermon on that day (Acts 2:16-18)!

Here is John the Baptist's prophecy:

> As for me, I baptize you with water for repentance, but He who is coming after me is mightier than I, and I am not fit to remove His sandals; He will baptize you with the Holy Spirit and fire. (Matthew 3:11)

But didn't the disciples already receive the Holy Spirit from Jesus when He breathed on them?

Yes!

Why would He give them the Holy Spirit a second time?

He didn't. Jesus only gave them the *indwelling of the Holy Spirit* when He breathed on them. That was not an *outpouring of the Holy Spirit*. The prophecies of Ezekiel 36 and Joel 2 we just looked at were two different prophecies with two different promises.

Ezekiel wrote about the new covenant in Jesus Christ that has God placing a new Spirit—the Holy Spirit—*within us*. That's what happened to the disciples in John 20:22 and what happens to us when we are saved (1 Corinthians 12:13).

This indwelling, though, does not bring power. It brings cleansing, a new heart and spirit, and removal of our heart of stone for a heart of flesh. With God's Spirit now in us, we will walk in His statutes and follow His ordinances and be continually made more and more righteous.

If the indwelling of the Holy Spirit we all receive at our salvation brought supernatural power, then *all* evangelicals,

Baptists, Methodists, Lutherans, and those in nondenominational churches—anyone saved by the blood of Jesus Christ—would be speaking in tongues and prophesying! They aren't. The reason? They overwhelmingly reject the baptism in the Holy Spirit.

Here's the difference: The indwelling of the Holy Spirit is about you getting more of the Holy Spirit, while *baptism in the Holy Spirit is about the Holy Spirit getting more of you!*

Through Joel's prophecy, then, God wasn't promising a second indwelling. Instead, He was promising a fresh, new *outpouring* of the Holy Spirit on *all mankind*. One that would include the power to prophesy, dream dreams, and see visions.

This is what most Christians and even most pastors and faith teachers don't understand. God not only sent His Son to give us eternal salvation through the new covenant, and the Holy Spirit to live *in* us for ongoing sanctification through that same new covenant, but He also promised to give a *separate and distinct outpouring of the Holy Spirit.*

It's this outpouring that brings power for witnessing and supernatural power for prophesying and building up the Body of Christ, as Paul wrote about in 1 Corinthians 12–14.

This is God's Word. You can either believe it and desire it or reject it.

Remember also, these promises aren't just for Israel, but they are for anyone born of flesh, anyone within the realm of "mankind."

In between Jesus breathing the Holy Spirit *into* His disciples in John 20:22 and ascending to heaven forty days later, He said to them:

> Gathering them together, He commanded them not to leave Jerusalem, but to wait for what the Father had promised, "Which," He said, "you heard of from Me; for John baptized with water, but you will be baptized with the Holy Spirit not many days from now… but you will receive power when the Holy Spirit has come upon you; and you shall be My witnesses both in Jerusalem and in all Judea, and Samaria, and as far as the remotest part of the earth." (Acts 1:4-5, 8)

Did you catch that? Jesus spoke to His disciples of three baptisms in total! We see their water baptism and their impending baptism in the Holy Spirit referenced in Acts 1:4-5, 8. But in between these two baptisms, Jesus baptized them with the indwelling Holy Spirit as we saw in John 20:22!

This is clear and unequivocal biblical proof that the disciples experienced three baptisms. In Chapter 7, we'll make the three baptisms for believers today just as clear.

After His resurrection, Jesus told the disciples to wait in Jerusalem and not begin work until they received the gift of the Holy Spirit from the Father. Jesus was their supernatural power while He was with them on earth. He knew they would not be able to witness, preach, perform miracles, or heal unless someone took His place. We humans (including the disciples) are not spiritually powerful on our own. We are weak and powerless. We need to be empowered by God, and He does this by having Jesus baptize us in the Holy Spirit. It is through the supernatural work of the Holy Spirit, or by God Himself directly, that healings and miracles happen, never by the effort of any man or woman.

The disciples would need to wait just ten days for this promise. They had no idea what was about to happen.

We covered the Day of Pentecost in Chapter 4, so we won't delve deep into it again here. But we do need to point out what happened from a baptism perspective.

The Day of Pentecost in AD 30 certainly began like any before it but would unfold like none since. Thousands of attendees would be transformed by the power of the Holy Spirit—the disciples first, led by Peter, then those in attendance via Peter's astonishing preaching:

> When the day of Pentecost had come, they were all together in one place. And suddenly a noise like a violent rushing wind came from heaven, and it filled the whole house where they were sitting. And tongues that looked like fire appeared to them, distributing themselves, and a tongue rested on each one of them. And they were all filled with the Holy Spirit and began to speak with different tongues, as the Spirit was giving them the ability to speak out. (Acts 2:1-4)

As Jesus promised and both Joel and John the Baptist prophesied, the disciples were indeed baptized with the Holy Spirit. He arrived from heaven with the noise of "a violent rushing wind" and "tongues that looked like fire."

This baptism was clearly different than either of their two previous baptisms—their water baptism and their salvation baptism with the indwelling of the Holy Spirit. Neither of those came with any power. But this third baptism gave the disciples the supernatural ability to speak in different languages, prophesy, and preach with power.

As we saw earlier, those thousands of Jews who'd gathered to learn the source of the noise heard the disciples speaking not in Hebrew or Aramaic or Greek (the languages local to Jerusalem) but in their own languages of the nations they traveled from:

> Now there were Jews residing in Jerusalem, devout men from every nation under heaven. And when this sound occurred, the crowd came together and they were bewildered, because each one of them was hearing them speak in his own language. They were amazed and astonished, saying, "Why, are not all these who are speaking Galileans? And how is it that we each hear them in our own language to which we were born? Parthians, Medes, and Elamites, and residents of Mesopotamia, Judea, and Cappadocia, Pontus and Asia, Phrygia and Pamphylia, Egypt and the parts of Libya around Cyrene, and visitors from Rome, both Jews and proselytes, Cretans and Arabs—we hear them speaking in our own tongues of the mighty deeds of God." And they all continued in amazement and great perplexity, saying to one another, "What does this mean?" But others were jeering and saying, "They are full of sweet wine!" (Acts 2:5-13)

Then we see Peter speaking up:

> But Peter, taking his stand with the other eleven, raised his voice and declared to them: "Men of Judea and all you who live in Jerusalem, know this, and pay attention to my words. For these people are not

drunk, as you assume, since it is only the third hour of the day; but this is what has been spoken through the prophet Joel:

> "'And it shall be in the last days,' God says,
> 'That I will pour out My Spirit on all mankind;
> And your sons and your daughters will prophesy,
> And your young men will see visions,
> And your old men will have dreams;
> And even on My male and female servants
> I will pour out My Spirit in those days,
> And they will prophesy.'" (Acts 2:14-18)

After that, Peter, now filled with the power of the Holy Spirit, preached:

> Men of Israel, listen to these words: Jesus the Nazarene, a Man attested to you by God with miracles and wonders and signs which God performed through Him in your midst, just as you yourselves know—this Man, delivered over by the predetermined plan and foreknowledge of God, you nailed to a cross by the hands of godless men and put Him to death. But God raised Him from the dead, putting an end to the agony of death, since it was impossible for Him to be held in its power.... Therefore, since He has been exalted at the right hand of God, and has received the promise of the Holy Spirit from the Father, He has poured out this which you both see and hear.... Therefore let

all the house of Israel know for certain that God has made Him both Lord and Christ—this Jesus whom you crucified. (Acts 2:22-24, 33, 36)

Look at what happened next:

> Now when they heard this, they were pierced to the heart, and said to Peter and the rest of the apostles, "Brothers, what are we to do?" Peter said to them, "Repent, and each of you be baptized in the name of Jesus Christ for the forgiveness of your sins; and you will receive the gift of the Holy Spirit. For the promise is for you and your children and for all who are far away, as many as the Lord our God will call to Himself." And with many other words he solemnly testified and kept on urging them, saying, "Be saved from this perverse generation!" So then, those who had received his word were baptized; and that day there were added about three thousand souls. They were continually devoting themselves to the apostles' teaching and to fellowship, to the breaking of bread and to prayer. (Acts 2:37-42)

Something had changed in Peter and the other disciples. One minute, they were in the upper room hiding from the religious Jews who'd killed their Jesus, and the next minute, they were speaking in new languages and preaching sermons that led three thousand fellow Jews to repent and be baptized.

The *only* difference was the arrival of the Holy Spirit, which both Joel and John the Baptist had prophesied, and which Jesus had promised. They now had the power to witness, preach, heal, and perform miracles on their own. They didn't do anything to receive this Spirit baptism except believe in who Jesus was—the Messiah, the Son of God, and then wait for Him to fall on them.

Two Down, One to Go

We've now covered the three baptisms of Jesus and of the disciples. Let's jump into the three baptisms that are available to believers today in this age of grace.

7
The Three Baptisms of Believers Today

IN THE PREVIOUS two chapters, we examined solid scriptural foundation to explain the three baptisms that Jesus and His disciples experienced. Believers today can and should experience three baptisms as well:

1. Salvation Baptism: We are baptized into the Body of Christ by the Holy Spirit.
2. Water Baptism: We are baptized in water by a disciple of Jesus.
3. Spirit Baptism: We are baptized in (or with) the Holy Spirit by Jesus.

In this chapter, we'll review these baptisms specifically as they relate to believers today and provide additional scriptural insights.

There are preachers, churches, and denominations today who teach that water baptism is not necessary for salvation. Which is biblical! Some, though, also teach that water baptisms serve no purpose at all or, worse, that they are not scriptural. While water baptisms are not necessary for salvation, nowhere does scripture call for an end to them.

Don't just believe what your pastor or church or denomination teaches—read and search the scriptures for yourself so *you* can discern the truth of what God says.

Water baptism is not necessary for salvation because it is a work of the flesh, of human effort, so it *cannot* aid in our salvation. Again, we are saved solely by grace alone and faith alone, not by any works on our part:

> For by grace you have been saved through faith; and this is not of yourselves, it is the gift of God; not a result of works, so that no one may boast. (Ephesians 2:8-9)

Let's also debunk a couple erroneous teachings about there being just "one baptism" for believers today:

> For there is one body and one Spirit, just as you have been called to one glorious hope for the future. There is one Lord, one faith, one baptism, one God and Father of all, who is over all, in all, and living through all. (Ephesians 4:4-6 NLT)

First, there are preachers and teachers who claim that the "one baptism" in this passage refers to water baptism. This cannot be correct. If there were only one baptism, it would be our baptism into the Body of Christ at our salvation:

> For by one Spirit we were all baptized into one body, whether Jews or Greeks, whether slaves or free, and we were all made to drink of one Spirit. (1 Corinthians 12:13)

Therefore, Ephesians 4:4-6 cannot refer to water baptism. It also doesn't restrict believers to just one baptism, but rather simply stresses that there is only *one baptism* required to come into unity with other believers via the *"one body"*—the Body of Christ. That can only happen through our salvation baptism, as shown in 1 Corinthians 12:13.

We only need to include the previous verses in Ephesians 4 to prove this:

> Therefore I, a prisoner for serving the Lord, beg you to lead a life worthy of your calling, for you have been called by God. Always be humble and gentle. Be patient with each other, making allowance for each other's faults because of your love. **Make every effort to keep yourselves united in the Spirit, binding yourselves together with peace.** For there is one body and one Spirit, just as you have been called to one glorious hope for the future. There is one Lord, one faith, one baptism, one God and Father of all, who is over all, in all, and living through all. (Ephesians 4:1-6 NLT)

This verse cannot be used to support the erroneous teaching that believers have only one baptism available to them.

Those who teach "one baptism" tell their followers that God did away with both water *and* Spirit baptisms in the first century. But *nothing* in scripture supports this idea. There are billions of Christians who have experienced beautiful water baptisms over the last two thousand years *and* who've also experienced supernatural power as the result of their baptism in the Holy Spirit.

Teaching believers that they have only one baptism available to them denies them the amazing opportunity to *symbolically* unite with Christ in His death, burial, and resurrection through water immersion. It's also an opportunity for new believers to declare publicly that they have died to self, their sins have been buried, and they have been raised to a new life in Christ Jesus. So beautiful!

Second, teaching one baptism also falsely instructs believers that they have all the power they need to live a Christian life, witness for Christ, and do their part to build up the Body of Christ. This teaching is not scriptural. It denies the words and ministry of the apostle Paul, specifically what he wrote to us in 1 Corinthians 12–14. And worse, it weakens believers and the entire Body of Christ.

Please do not believe everything your pastor says or whatever *anyone* says or writes or posts on social media! Respect biblically accurate pastors and teachers but take even what they say straight to the Word of God and determine *for yourself* whether their teachings line up with scripture or not.

Ephesians 4:4-6 clearly indicates that Paul is referring to the *one* Body of Christ that we are baptized into by the *one* Holy Spirit at our moment of salvation. There is no mention of water in these verses nor elsewhere in Ephesians 4. This passage simply tells us that, for this church age and age of grace, we are called to one body and one hope by one Holy Spirit through our faith in Jesus Christ. That's it. These verses do not call for an end to water baptism, nor do they deny baptism in the Holy Spirit. Paul was merely emphasizing the need for every believer to live out the unity they were called to in the Body of Christ.

Let's just go ahead and throw the baby (baptisms) out with the bathwater: infant baptism brings no spiritual benefit. If water baptism is not necessary for salvation, then infant baptism *cannot* bring salvation either. It cannot bring anything to the child or to the parents. Salvation is a choice a person makes of their own free will, not something that can be chosen for them by someone else.

Salvation is a decision of the heart, not of the parents nor of a church. Infant baptism was created by man and taught as doctrine with zero biblical foundation. Those who practice infant baptism are not following God and His Word but instead following the doctrine of a church defined and built by man.

We learned in earlier chapters that "baptism" means immersion—literally a dunking or soaking. Sprinkling water on a child is not immersion. At best, it fulfills a church tradition or mandate (which has nothing to do with salvation) and provides comfort for the parents and grandparents, though a truly false comfort.

As well, countless people of all ages have chosen to be water-baptized *without* a previous heart decision for Christ. They leave the water believing they are saved and sealed for eternity. But they're just simply wet.

I personally watched over a dozen people be water-baptized on a Sunday morning a few years ago. The church was planning on just a handful of baptisms for specific individuals who had already been saved. After those individuals were immersed, the pastor asked if anyone else wanted to be baptized. People young and old raised their hands and stepped up to be dunked. No one was asked if they were saved—if they believed that Jesus died for them, was buried, and rose again. One by one, they simply stepped into the water and were fully immersed as others cheered.

How many individuals were baptized that morning without understanding what they were doing? How many left believing, and still believing, that because they were baptized in water, they were saved? As with infant baptism, it means nothing. It provides an eternally false security in salvation. Water baptisms don't save anyone today in this age of grace.

Now, while most believers have received both their salvation and water baptisms, they unfortunately have not heard about the Holy Spirit baptism available to them. Their pastor or denomination may dismiss it as heresy or unbiblical, but, as proven throughout this book, it is fully biblical and for today.

Let's dive a little deeper into each of the three baptisms of believers.

1) Salvation Baptism

At our salvation baptism (a believer's first baptism) we are baptized into the Body of Christ by the Holy Spirit. In that moment, we also receive the indwelling of the Holy Spirit:

> For by one Spirit we were all baptized into one body, whether Jews or Greeks, whether slaves or free, and we were all made to drink of one Spirit. (1 Corinthians 12:13)

Here are the amazing gifts God gives us as new believers in Jesus:

- We become a new creation in Christ (2 Corinthians 5:17).
- We become righteous in God's eyes (2 Corinthians 5:21).
- We are "justified" by God, which means He sees us *just as if we never sinned* (Romans 5:1).
- We are placed into the Body of Christ (1 Corinthians 12:13).
- Our sins—past, present, and future—are wiped away, forever forgiven, and forever forgotten (Hebrews 10:17-18).
- We receive a spiritual gift(s) to serve the Body of Christ (Romans 12:3-8).
- We are sealed by the Holy Spirit, which means we have the gift of everlasting life (Ephesians 1:13; 4:30).
- The Holy Spirit dwells in us (Romans 8:9, 11; 1 Corinthians 3:16; 6:19; Galatians 4:6; et al.).
- We are sanctified—set apart as holy (Romans 6:6; 1 Corinthians 6:19; Ephesians 4:24; et al.).
- The Holy Spirit then *continually* sanctifies us away from sin and toward righteousness (John 16:8; Philippians 1:6; Galatians 5:16; et al.).
- We receive the fruit of the Holy Spirit (which

> flows from within us out to the world) and we
> lose our fruit of the flesh (Galatians 5:22-23).

Our salvation baptism does not bring us power, though. That only happens at our Spirit baptism. We are simply indwelled with the Holy Spirit who will be our helper, comforter, and guide, helping us to continually grow in Christ, grow in holiness and righteousness, and mature in the Word.

It is important to understand that we only need to be saved once. And that means we do not need to ask God to forgive our sins, nor do we need to continue asking Him to forgive our sins going forward.

Jesus *already* paid the price for us—for every one of our past, present, and future sins. To continually ask for forgiveness for each new sin means we would be nailing Jesus to the cross over and over and over.

It is finished. He paid it all:

> So now there is **no condemnation** for those who belong to Christ Jesus. And because you belong to him, the power of the life-giving Spirit has freed you from the power of sin that leads to death. (Romans 8:1-2 NLT)

> Therefore if anyone is in Christ, this person is a new creation; the old things passed away; behold, new things have come. (2 Corinthians 5:17)

God is not going to revoke these verses from you each time you sin and then take you back only after you ask for forgiveness. No. He said you are forgiven. You are no longer condemned. You have been set free from the power of sin. You are a new creation in Christ Jesus.

Also know that, since we are sealed in Christ for all of eternity, we *cannot* lose our salvation. God is not going to give you the gift of eternal life and then take it away from you. You can fully trust God in this. Rest in His promise of total forgiveness of your sins and gracious gift of eternal life.

Paul described exactly what happens in our moment of salvation. First, though, a passage from his letter to the Colossians:

> When you came to Christ, you were "circumcised," but not by a physical procedure. Christ performed a spiritual circumcision—the cutting away of your sinful nature. For you were buried with Christ when you were baptized. And with him you were raised to new life because you trusted the mighty power of God, who raised Christ from the dead. You were dead because of your sins and because your sinful nature was not yet cut away. Then God made you alive with Christ, **for he forgave all our sins**. He canceled the record of the charges against us and took it away by nailing it to the cross. (Colossians 2:11-14 NLT)

Verse 12's "when you were baptized" is not referring to water baptism but to the spiritual baptism we experience at our salvation (as shown in 1 Corinthians 12:13). We get to experience this spiritual baptism because Jesus Himself *physically* died, was *physically* buried, and was *physically* raised to new life. It's like God allows us to "piggyback" on Christ's own death, burial, and resurrection.

Verse 11 confirms that our involvement is not through physical water baptism but spiritual—just as our circumcision at salvation isn't a physical cutting away but a spiritual cutting away of our sinful nature. We do not need to physically die, be buried, and be raised again. Jesus already did that for us. We also do not need to be physically baptized in water to be saved either. We are saved the moment we believe in what Jesus did for us—no other works are needed, no words, no prayer required.

So, in our moment of salvation, we die, are buried, and are raised with Christ in His *physical* death, burial, and resurrection. Water baptism has no power because it is not a spiritual act but a physical human act. It is also a "work," and we are not saved by works but by faith alone in Christ alone. Water baptism simply represents a physical expression of our spiritual decision to believe in Christ's full work of the cross.

Paul reiterated this same message in his epistle to the Romans. Here again, this baptism is our spiritual salvation baptism, not our water baptism:

> Or have you forgotten that when we were joined with Christ Jesus in baptism, we joined him in his death? For we died and were buried with Christ by baptism. And just as Christ was raised from the dead by the glorious power of the Father, now we also may live new lives. Since we have been united with him in his death, we will also be raised to life as he was. We know that our old sinful selves were crucified with Christ so that sin might lose its power in our lives. We are

no longer slaves to sin. For when we died with Christ we were set free from the power of sin. (Romans 6:3-7 NLT)

In our salvation baptism, God joined us with His Son's own physical death, burial, and resurrection. That is when our old, sinful self died and was buried:

> I have been crucified with Christ; and it is no longer I who live, but Christ lives in me; and the life which I now live in the flesh I live by faith in the Son of God, who loved me and gave Himself up for me. (Galatians 2:20)

You are no longer a sinner. That was your old self. You are forgiven and free because you are now in Christ. You are also now a child of God.

You and I still sin, but that's not *who* we are—because of *whose* we are, we are no longer sinners.

Jesus cut away our sin and sinful nature. And because of our faith in God the Father, He raised us to new life with His Son. We can be raised to new life because He forgave all our sins. They are gone. Forgiven. Forgotten. Forever nailed to the cross.

We are saved. Sealed for eternity. Delivered forever from the consequences of sin and death!

2) Water Baptism

Here are the three most important points to understand about water baptisms:

1. *They are not necessary for salvation.* Salvation is solely by the grace of God + our faith + nothing else. Water baptisms are a work of the flesh. We are not saved by our own works. Works glorify us as humans and invite us to boast about our part in salvation. We have no part. The work of salvation rests fully on God's grace and Christ's work on the cross.
2. *Water baptisms are still biblical today.* Even though they are not required for salvation in this age of grace, they are recommended and a wonderful experience. This is certainly true for new believers, but as a parent who's witnessed a child be baptized, it's just as amazing and emotional for witnesses as well. (Yes, I cried.) Nowhere in scripture are we commanded to stop performing water baptisms, nor are we commanded to perform them as a requirement for salvation.
3. *Water baptisms can be performed by any believer.* Pastors are not the only ones who can water-baptize new believers. Any follower of Jesus can perform a baptism. Parents can baptize their children. A spouse can baptize their husband or wife. Siblings, grandparents, friends—anyone saved by the blood of Jesus can perform a water baptism on a new believer.

But didn't Jesus give us the Great Commission where He commanded His disciples to go into all the world, preach the gospel, and baptize people?

Yes, He did!

But that was written to Jews during Jesus's earthly ministry. Remember that He and John the Baptist were preaching the gospel of the kingdom of God: "Repent and be baptized." That gospel message isn't for us today. We are not saved by repenting and being baptized in water. That was for Jews during Christ's earthly ministry. The gospel that saves today in this age of grace is 1 Corinthians 15:1-4.

The Great Commission that Jesus gave to the disciples in Matthew 28:19-20 and Mark 16:15-18 was for Jews, not Gentiles. And this is easily provable.

First, we have already shown that Jesus Himself said that He "was sent only to the lost sheep of the house of Israel" (Matthew 15:24).

He also told His disciples to not go to Gentiles nor to Samaritans, but "go to the lost sheep of the house of Israel" (Matthew 10:5-6).

Jesus never changed those directives, so they were still valid up through His crucifixion, and really until He called the apostle Paul.

Also, if we look at the Great Commission as recorded in Matthew's gospel, it is very clear that Jesus's words were not for Gentiles in that day nor for us today in this age of grace; they were solely for Jews of His day:

> Go, therefore, and make disciples of all the nations, baptizing them in the name of the Father and the Son and the Holy Spirit, teaching them to follow all that I commanded you; and behold, I am with you always, to the end of the age. (Matthew 28:19-20)

If we were to follow all that Jesus commanded His disciples, we would be very confused by the many contradictions between what Jesus commanded for the Jews of His day versus what the apostle Paul wrote for you and me to follow in this age of grace.

This is exactly the situation that most pastors, teachers, churches, denominations, and Christians find themselves in today: confused!

If you were to follow the Great Commission, you would also need to follow the Ten Commandments (which you can't—only Jesus could) and the other 603 Mosaic laws that Jesus and His fellow Jews followed in that time.

Remember, Jesus's last words on the cross were, "It is finished!" (John 19:30). That is the moment He fulfilled the law and the prophets. He would later reveal to the apostle Paul the gospel of grace by which you and I are saved today.

It is important to read and understand Paul's letters—Romans through Philemon—if you truly want to know what it means to follow and be a disciple of Jesus today. If you don't know what Paul wrote, then you are defaulting to being a follower of what Jesus taught during His earthly ministry, as recorded in the gospels of Matthew, Mark, Luke, and John. This means you are choosing to follow the law rather than live under the grace of God. At best, you live in confusion by mixing law with grace; at worst, you reject the grace of God to follow the law.

This is one of Paul's primary messages in Romans and Galatians:

> Sin is no longer your master, for you no longer live under the requirements of the law. Instead, you live under the freedom of God's grace. (Romans 6:14 NLT)

If you truly believe the Great Commission is for today, then here is a command from Jesus you must follow:

> For if you forgive other people for their offenses, your heavenly Father will also forgive you. But if you do not forgive other people, then your Father will not forgive your offenses. (Matthew 6:14-15)

Is it a good idea to forgive others? Absolutely! But if you want to follow Jesus's command in this verse, then you must forgive others every single time, and if you don't, God the Father won't forgive you. And you must forgive others *first* before God will forgive your offenses.

This is *not* the gospel of grace that we live under today! The gospel that Jesus preached in this passage is a totally separate gospel from what He gave to Paul for us today.

Both gospels are from Jesus, though. One was for Jews during His earthly ministry, the other for all people (Jew and Gentile) during this age of grace.

Here is how Paul described forgiveness for Christians in this age of grace:

> Be kind to one another, compassionate, forgiving each other, just as God in Christ also has forgiven you. (Ephesians 4:32)

Do you see the difference? It's amazing! It's also contradictory.

Jesus commanded the Jews to forgive others *first* or God would not forgive them.

Through Paul, Jesus now tells us that, in this age of grace *after His crucifixion*, God has *already* forgiven us. Therefore, we need to always be kind, compassionate, and forgiving toward others, regardless of how others treat us.

That is the difference between the age of the law and the prophets and the age of grace and the church.

It's also the difference between Christ's earthly ministry before His death on the cross and the ministry He gave to Paul in Acts 9—as well as the difference between Christ's gospel of the kingdom that He, John the Baptist, and the disciples preached and the gospel of grace that He revealed to the apostle Paul.

Here is another command Jesus gave to the Jews listening to His Sermon on the Mount:

> Therefore you shall be perfect, as your heavenly Father is perfect. (Matthew 5:48)

Good luck following this command! It would certainly be difficult (*impossible*) to follow. Jews were expected to be perfect, though. They had to follow the Ten Commandments, the 603 other laws in the Torah, all laws that the Pharisees made up on a whim, and all Roman laws on top of these!

In this age of grace, instead of trying to follow Christ's command to be perfect, here is what Paul calls us to, a message he received from Jesus:

> I don't mean to say that I have already achieved these things or that I have already reached perfection. But I press on to possess that perfection for which Christ Jesus first possessed me. No, dear brothers and sisters, I have not achieved it, but I focus on this one thing: Forgetting the past and looking forward to what lies ahead, I press on to reach the end of the race and receive the heavenly prize for which God, through Christ Jesus, is calling us. (Philippians 3:12-14 NLT)

Instead of striving for perfection, Paul calls believers to acknowledge that we're *not* perfect. And, better yet, to not even look back at our failures, but to press on toward the goal of the heavenly prize to which God has called us. In the previous verses of Philippians 3, Paul provided a truly vivid understanding of his own astonishing journey from law to grace:

> I was circumcised when I was eight days old. I am a pure-blooded citizen of Israel and a member of the tribe of Benjamin—a real Hebrew if there ever was one! I was a member of the Pharisees, who demand the strictest obedience to the Jewish law. I was so zealous that I harshly persecuted the church. And as for righteousness, I obeyed the law without fault. **I once thought these things were valuable, but now I consider them worthless because of what Christ has done.** (Philippians 3:5-7 NLT)

Are you living under the law or under the grace of God? Know that He sent His Son to die so you can be set free from the law that shackles you to sin and death and blocks your freedom in Christ.

Paul not only preached the grace of God over bondage to the law, but he lived out that transformation from law to grace—and brutally so (see 2 Corinthians 11:24-27, for example).

If Jesus can transform Paul, He can transform anyone—and from out of the most desperate of situations.

A final command you would need to follow is the Great Commission itself. You would need to go and make disciples of all the nations. This doesn't mean just evangelizing, though. There is a big difference between the two. Evangelizing is not the same as making disciples, and making disciples is not simply evangelizing. This was especially true in first-century Judaism.

Either can occur first, but the outcome should always be new disciples, not getting people saved and moving on. Making disciples means walking with someone long enough to grow them into a faithful follower of Jesus. (Or in Hebrew tradition, develop them into "replicas" of the rabbi himself.)

This was the context of "making disciples" when Matthew and Mark wrote their gospels.

Jesus was a rabbi. He called His disciples to follow Him. So, they did just that—they left everything to follow Him so they could become like Him. They did this full-time for three years. That was the meaning of being a disciple at that time, to follow the teacher full-time to learn all that the teacher knew and how to behave exactly like them.

You would then need to baptize people in water in the name of the Father and the Son and the Holy Spirit. And then you would need to teach them to follow all that Jesus commanded His disciples: commands like forgiving others or God won't forgive you, being perfect, and making disciples of all nations.

Let's look at how Mark recorded the Great Commission to see if he makes it any easier on us:

> And He said to them, "Go into all the world and preach the gospel to all creation. **The one who has believed and has been baptized will be saved**; but the one who has not believed will be condemned. These signs will accompany those who have believed: in My name they will cast out demons, they will speak with new tongues; they will pick up serpents, and if they drink any deadly poison, it will not harm them; they will lay hands on the sick, and they will recover." (Mark 16:15-18)

Nope. I don't think Mark made this any easier.

Do you see the issue with following Jesus's Great Commission?

He *requires* baptism for salvation. We are not saved by works today but by grace alone + faith alone + nothing else. Jesus was preaching a different gospel here than our gospel for today.

Have you ever led anyone to Christ? Did they begin casting out demons, speaking with new tongues, picking up serpents and drinking deadly poison without harm, and healing those who are sick?

Who do you know that is fulfilling the Great Commission today? Who do you know that is following Jesus's commands that He gave here? Any individual? Church? Mission? Ministry?

No one is.

First, when someone is saved today, we don't immediately baptize them in water. If we had to follow this command, no one would be fully saved *until* they were baptized in water. That could take days, weeks, months, years, or it may never happen! This would leave people at risk of dying before they could be water-baptized and fully saved.

Second, all that Jesus listed—from casting out demons to healing the sick—were signs… for *Jews*. Gentiles today don't need signs to believe. We also don't perform signs once we believe. Jews needed signs to believe, and that was what Jesus referred to in Mark 16. We, though, are saved by faith:

> For indeed Jews ask for signs and Greeks search for wisdom; but we preach Christ crucified, to Jews a stumbling block, and to Gentiles foolishness, but to those who are the called, both Jews and Greeks, Christ the power of God and the wisdom of God. (1 Corinthians 1:22-24)

Do you see the difference between Jesus's earthly kingdom ministry and the ministry that He gave to Paul? It's simply law versus grace. It's the gospel of the kingdom of God preached to Jews versus the gospel of grace by which we are saved today. Old covenant versus new covenant. Pre-crucifixion versus post-crucifixion.

Which gospel do you wish to live under? The gospel of the kingdom, which includes following the law, or the gospel of grace?

Both are of Christ. You can't have both, though. You can't mix them. That's what most believers, churches, and denominations do today. They're unwittingly mixing law and grace and confusing everyone.

I choose Jesus Christ. I choose to fully believe in my heart what He did for me on the cross. He shed His blood and died, was buried, and rose again three days later. I choose this age of grace and His gospel of grace. And I choose to follow the teachings He revealed to the apostle Paul.

Once I understood the gospel of grace and age of grace versus the gospel of the kingdom and age of the law, scripture came to life for me. It finally made sense. I clearly see now what Jesus was teaching *to Jews* in the gospels versus what Paul taught in his epistles. And I see the book of Acts for what it is: transitional and historical.

When I read the Bible now or hear a sermon, I can understand what passages are for me today and what were for Jews prior to Christ's death, burial, and resurrection.

I love Jesus! I still learn from His teachings, but I now understand that not everything He said was meant for me or for believers today.

When I first became a Christian at age nineteen, I couldn't get enough of Matthew 6. I especially needed Jesus's lessons on "not worrying." Yes, that teaching was to Jews only in Christ's day (because Gentiles were idol worshippers and far from God). However, there is nothing that sets it apart as solely for Israel today. I'm blessed to have read it, applied its teaching, and allowed it to transform my heart, mind, and life.

I love Jesus and praise and worship Him for what He did for me on the cross. I believe that He bled and died for my sins, was buried, and rose again three days later. *That is the gospel that saves!*

And I believe that all my sins were fully covered and forgiven the exact moment He died—*not* in 1981 when I was saved. That is just when I heard the Good News, understood it, wanted it, and chose to believe it.

Nothing from Christ's earthly ministry saves today. Nothing. Not everything He said in the gospels is for us today. Believing this will only confuse you and leave you with a weak and powerless Christian walk. Unfortunately, this is the situation most churches and believers are in today.

Jews during Jesus's earthly ministry (and into the early period of Acts) were required to be water-baptized for the forgiveness of their sins. Water baptism is no longer required for forgiveness or salvation. *Our sins were forgiven by the shed blood of Jesus two thousand years ago, not by any immersing, dunking, or sprinkling with water today.*

While water baptism is not required at all, it is still a beautiful experience both for the new believer and for witnesses. I highly recommend everyone be water-baptized after choosing to believe in what Jesus did for them on the cross. But know that it is a symbolic ceremony only, giving new believers the chance to publicly profess their new life in Jesus.

3) Spirit Baptism

When you get Spirit-baptized, you receive the power of God to witness for Christ, so others can know what He did for you. Your witness *is* preaching the gospel—and preaching the gospel saves. You also receive the supernatural power of the

Holy Spirit to work His spiritual gifts through you to grow and build up the Body of Christ.

As Paul informs us, the Holy Spirit demonstrates God's power by preaching and witnessing through us:

> And my message and my preaching were very plain. Rather than using clever and persuasive speeches, I relied only on the power of the Holy Spirit. I did this so you would trust not in human wisdom but in the power of God. (1 Corinthians 2:4-5 NLT)

We cannot do it alone. We need to be filled with the Holy Spirit—through Spirit baptism—to give us the power to witness for Jesus, to build up other believers, to build up the Body of Christ, and to pray to God in our "private prayer language," as we looked at earlier.

Jesus—the Lord and Savior of the world—was introduced to us in *all four gospels* as the One who would baptize with the Holy Spirit (Matthew 3:11; Mark 1:8; Luke 3:16; John 1:33). Matthew and Luke included that He would baptize with "the Holy Spirit and with fire."

And Jesus Himself promised this baptism to His disciples:

> Gathering them together, He commanded them not to leave Jerusalem, but to wait for what the Father had promised, "Which," He said, "you heard of from Me; for John baptized with water, but you will be baptized with the Holy Spirit not many days from now.... but you will receive power when the Holy Spirit has

come upon you; and you shall be My witnesses both in Jerusalem and in all Judea, and Samaria, and as far as the remotest part of the earth." (Acts 1:4-5, 8)

Jesus's promise came through ten days later, on the Day of Pentecost. But His promise was not just for those disciples and Jews! Again, here is what Peter said immediately after his own Spirit baptism when many thought he was drunk:

But Peter, taking his stand with the other eleven, raised his voice and declared to them: "Men of Judea and all you who live in Jerusalem, know this, and pay attention to my words. For these people are not drunk, as you assume, since it is only the third hour of the day; but this is what has been spoken through the prophet Joel:

"'And it shall be in the last days,' God says,
'That **I will pour out My Spirit on all mankind**;
And your sons and your daughters will prophesy,
And your young men will see visions,
And your old men will have dreams;
And even on My male and female servants
I will pour out My Spirit in those days,
And they will prophesy.'" (Acts 2:14-18)

Peter was very clear about what Joel had prophesied—that God said He would pour out His Spirit *"on all mankind."* Later, Peter told everyone that this promise of the Holy Spirit was for those in the future, not just those in attendance that day in Jerusalem:

> This promise is to you, to your children, and to those far away—all who have been called by the Lord our God. (Acts 2:39 NLT)

Peter did not mean "far away" as in distance, but far away as in time, in the future. This promise was and is to *all of mankind* even to those *far into the future*. God is including you and me in His promise of the Holy Spirit!

Baptism in the Holy Spirit allows the Holy Spirit to fill us—not just indwell us but fill us—with His supernatural gifts. That is another amazing topic, but one we will not delve into in this book. Paul describes these gifts and how they build up the Body of Christ in 1 Corinthians 12.

Those baptized with the Holy Spirit also receive a private prayer language. This is a controversial topic, but it shouldn't be. Here is the verse that describes this very special language God gifted us to speak directly with Him:

> For if you have the ability to speak in tongues [*in unknown languages*], you will be talking only to God, since people won't be able to understand you. You will be speaking by the power of the Spirit, but it will all be mysterious. (1 Corinthians 14:2 NLT)

As I mentioned in the Preface, you will need to do *something* with this verse. Paul is the apostle to the Gentiles, even today, which includes you and me. So, this verse is written to you, and it is for you. Please don't ignore it. Study it to understand it, but then either reject it or believe it.

Once you see and believe God for this amazing gift of prayer, this passage in Romans becomes clear and meaningful:

> And the Holy Spirit helps us in our weakness. For example, we don't know what God wants us to pray for. But the Holy Spirit prays for us with groanings that cannot be expressed in words. And the Father who knows all hearts knows what the Spirit is saying, for the Spirit pleads for us believers in harmony with God's own will. (Romans 8:26-27 NLT)

So, all the babbling baby talk and nonsensical syllables you've heard coming out of the mouths of those crazy people (usually in Pentecostal or charismatic churches) is actually the Holy Spirit speaking or praying or singing on their behalf. And He's praying the perfect prayer for those individuals because they don't always know what to pray for, but God's Spirit in them does.

Now, I will say that people do fake speaking in tongues, but that's an issue between them and God. My issue is when people pray or speak in tongues in public. This is not scriptural at all. It's distracting and many are simply showing off. They are honoring themselves versus honoring God.

Please know that once you are baptized in the Holy Spirit, you will *not* start behaving like a crazy person in public or even in private. (Unless that's already your natural personality!) I promise you that won't happen. That is *not* how the Holy Spirit behaves nor how He wants us to behave. We are in control of our words, and God is a God of order, not of chaos:

> For God is not a God of confusion, but of peace. (1 Corinthians 14:33)

Finally, spirit baptisms, as with water baptisms, are not required for salvation. Even though they are optional, they are biblical and will dramatically change your faith and your life.

Baptism in the Holy Spirit is biblical and for today. We know that Paul is the writer of 1 Corinthians 12–14 and that he is our apostle for this age of grace. Jesus revealed these teachings to him, and the Holy Spirit ensured they were included in the Bible.

How and when these powers and gifts come upon a believer after their Spirit baptism is different for every individual. I have friends who went years before experiencing their private prayer language. And many have never experienced the Holy Spirit manifesting a supernatural gift in them or through them. Or they didn't realize it was the Holy Spirit at work.

I know believers who say the Holy Spirit works one of His supernatural gifts in their life so often it feels like they walk full-time in that gift.

Since my Spirit baptism in 2017, I have experienced His supernatural gifts, specifically word of wisdom, word of knowledge, and distinguishing of spirits. I also experienced gifts of healing in a profound way, though I did not respond well to it. I was visiting a friend in the hospital. I felt *and* heard a roaring fire inside me. I had never experienced anything like that before. I didn't know what to do with it, though, so I kept it to myself. Looking back, I should have laid my hands on him and asked God to heal him. That is a very real example of the Holy Spirit manifesting His power at His will, but, unfortunately, a very real example of quenching the Holy Spirit as well.

My own wait for a prayer language was a few months. I will say that I was skeptical at first, so that likely played into the delay. I tried forcing it to happen, but that felt fake and inauthentic. I just gave up and told God if He wanted me to have this prayer gift, I would welcome it.

Then, one night, these "sounds" just poured out of my mouth for several seconds. I was not trying or even thinking about praying. It just happened.

I still experience unexpected praying in tongues on occasion, but I usually initiate it on my own when I feel the need. I don't force it, though. I just as much enjoy speaking to God in my own words that I understand, but there is something truly amazing about knowing the Holy Spirit is praying the perfect will of God on my behalf. Just wow.

I also don't pray in tongues in public or even at church. On the rare occasion I do, I pray in my mind, or I whisper.

Paul is clear about maintaining order in the church and not giving outsiders reason to think we're crazy if everyone is speaking in "unknown languages." He tells us that praying in tongues to God edifies the individual—it builds up the one doing the praying.

The Power of the Holy Spirit in Us

Everyone is different, so the Holy Spirit works in and through us in unique ways. Some of His workings begin immediately after Spirit baptism, while some are delayed for reasons only God knows.

I have experienced different seasons of His gifts. Sometimes, distinguishing of spirits is strong, and then it's not. There are times that He's quiet and other times He's more active in me.

The following are some highlights of my experience after I was baptized in the Holy Spirit in 2017.

Hearing music: My first experience of the Holy Spirit's power working in me happened on a Sunday morning just two weeks after my baptism. I woke up and heard angels singing. I had *never* experienced anything like that before. It was a beautiful experience and one I didn't want to end. I tried lying there, very still, hoping the singing would continue. After about a minute, though, it faded away. I've heard hundreds of amazing songs now in my dreams, most everyone has been original. I try to force myself awake and write the words down, but often fail to accomplish either.

Prophetic dreams: Although I already had a vibrant dream life, my dreams became more real, vivid, and prophetic. Now, prophetic does not always mean "foretelling" of a future-oriented event. In fact, it rarely does. The word *prophetic* simply refers to a message from God. That's all. Nothing more. These messages from God can be future-oriented but more often relate to current situations in life where God is giving a message of insight or guidance about a situation.

I have received one future-oriented prophetic dream since my Spirit baptism. That's it: just one. However, I have received from God many prophetic dreams that have guided and directed me in my life and Christian walk.

For example, a couple years ago, God scolded me in a dream after I had not handled a situation with a friend appropriately. God showed me that I was supposed to be their protector, but instead I failed to be that for them. The next day, I shared the dream with my friend and apologized. Our relationship was strengthened because of that "prophetic" dream.

The more we pay attention to and obey God and the Holy Spirit within us, whether through prophetic dreams or however He speaks, the more responsibility He is willing to give us and the more He is willing to use us to grow His kingdom.

Distinguishing (or discerning) of spirits: This is the gift the Holy Spirit works in me most often. He lets me know the source of a spirit, whether in a person, a situation, or an object (like a book, movie, store, etc.). Any spirit could be of God, a heavenly (angelic) spirit, a human (fleshly) spirit, or demonic spirit.

For example, I've attempted to enter stores only to have the Holy Spirit stop me. I've been in coffee shops when someone walks in and I immediately know they carry a demonic spirit. And He reveals false preachers, teachers, and prophets to me as well.

What I receive is like a "knowing" that someone or something is of God, angelic, fleshly, or demonic. I often mess this up, though, by allowing my own perspective, desires, or feelings to hijack what He is trying to communicate to me.

This is just a quick peak at the type of relationship I've had with God, Jesus, and the Holy Spirit since my Spirit baptism. I certainly wish I'd started here in 1981, but I'm so blessed to be living it now. I truly hope the same blessing for you!

Up Next: Application!

You've made it through the Foundation and Core chapters of the book… Way to go!

The final three chapters will help you apply what you've learned, whether for yourself or for leading others to salvation, water baptism, or baptism in the Holy Spirit.

APPLICATION CHAPTERS

8

How to Be Truly Saved

ONCE CONCEIVED AND born, humans live on, continuing into eternity. Even after we die. When we die, we persist, we still exist. Our physical body might go into the ground, but our soul and spirit will live on forever. Somewhere.

Every person will either spend the remainder of their eternity in heaven or in the lake of fire. It's our choice. Not God's. Not anyone else's.

Salvation is God's way of reconciling us back to Him, as we were originally before Adam sinned in the garden. By believing in what God's Son did for us on the cross, we can be saved from our sinful selves while still on earth and then later saved from spending the remainder of eternity in the lake of fire.

God is clear about how we can be truly and confidently saved today in this age of grace. We are saved by the gospel, the Good News of 1 Corinthians 15:1-4, which Jesus revealed to the apostle Paul and which Paul then revealed to the world—and it bears repeating here again:

> Let me now remind you, dear brothers and sisters, of the Good News I preached to you before. You welcomed it then, and you still stand firm in it. **It is this Good News that saves you** if you continue to believe the message I told you—unless, of course, you believed something that was never true in the first place. I passed on to you what was most important and what had also been passed on to me. **Christ died for our sins, just as the Scriptures said. He was buried, and he was raised from the dead on the third day, just as the Scriptures said.** (NLT)

There is only one condition required for salvation: Being separated from God and in need of a Savior. This is the human condition we all inherit from Adam.

Adam's sin not only separated himself from God but you and me as well. The *only* way to be in relationship with Him again is through the blood of His Son, Jesus Christ.

When we are truly saved, the Holy Spirit enters us and sanctifies us (sets us apart as holy) and continues to sanctify us—change us, transform us—toward greater righteousness and holiness.

No prayer is required—no prayer on your part or by a pastor or anyone else. Nowhere in the Bible does God or Jesus give us a prayer of salvation to pray. Nowhere. Throughout scripture, God tells us that only belief (faith) leads to righteousness, which means being in right standing with Him. In this age of grace, it is faith *alone* that saves.

You'll notice also that nowhere did Paul say Gentiles need to confess sins or repent. Nowhere! These are all human works.

We are not saved by our own works but solely by the work of Jesus Christ on the cross, by the grace of God through faith:

> For by grace you have been saved through faith; and this is not of yourselves, it is the gift of God; not a result of works, so that no one may boast. (Ephesians 2:8-9)

Biblical repentance has nothing to do with sin. It simply means, "change of mind." That's it. And repentance was for Jews only in the days of Jesus, and part of the kingdom message that He and John the Baptist preached.

Jews who repented weren't changing their mind about sin, but about the path they were walking, a path far from the God of their fathers—Abraham, Isaac, and Jacob. Since Gentiles weren't of Jewish lineage, they couldn't change their mind about God because they never knew Him!

The prophet Isaiah described it well:

> All of us, like sheep, have gone astray,
> Each of us has turned to his own way; (Isaiah 53:6a)

Jews were called to change their mind and turn back to God. Jesus also declared it in Revelation 2, in His warning to the church at Ephesus:

> But I have this against you, that you have left your first love [God]. Therefore, remember from where you have fallen, and repent, and do the deeds you did at

> first; or else I am coming to you and I will remove your lampstand from its place—unless you repent. (Revelation 2:4-5)

Christ already died for you and me. He already shed His blood for us. We just need to believe in what He's already accomplished. *That* is repentance today—changing one's mind about Jesus, going from unbelief in Him to belief:

> For the kind of sorrow God wants us to experience leads us away from sin and results in salvation. There's no regret for that kind of sorrow. But worldly sorrow, which lacks repentance, results in spiritual death. (2 Corinthians 7:10)

Once again, repentance simply means, "change of mind." Believing means believing, which encompasses faith and trust as well.

Repentance and confession are works. They are *not* required for salvation in this current age of grace, nor are they required to *keep* salvation. Jesus has already paid that full price. And we are sealed for eternity.

Think of it this way: If you're not saved and walking a bad path, living a life of sin, God does not tell you to first clean up your act and then you can be saved. No! He also doesn't tell you to confess all your sins and then seek salvation. This is *not* God's wonderful gospel of grace for today. Jesus *already* died for the sins of the whole world, including yours. We just need to believe in what He has already accomplished—nothing more.

You also don't need to be water-baptized to be saved. You don't need to follow the Ten Commandments to be saved. You don't need to repent. And you don't need to confess your sins. It is done. Finished. You only need to believe:

> But God demonstrates His own love toward us, in that while we were still sinners, Christ died for us. (Romans 5:8)

Can you still say a prayer? Absolutely! But know that the words of your prayer or the words someone else prays over you do not save you. Only your wholehearted belief in what Christ did for you on the cross can save you. Your words will simply express the belief you now hold in your heart.

You are also sealed for all of eternity by the Holy Spirit, and you receive the other gifts God has for you, which we discussed in Chapter 7:

> In Him, you also, after listening to the message of truth, the gospel of your salvation—having also believed, you were sealed in Him with the Holy Spirit of the promise. (Ephesians 1:13)

Also know that you do not *ever* need to be saved again. No scripture exists to support the claim that you can lose your salvation. You are sealed for eternity, and no one can take that gift away from you.

But how can you be certain that you are saved and sealed for eternity?

By faith! Faith that God, full of grace, sent His Son to die for you. He also said (through Paul) that to be saved, you only need to believe in His Son's death, burial, and resurrection. You believe by faith and are saved by faith because of the grace of God. Nothing more! Trust God that His Word is true. He is faithful.

If you have not been saved or you're not sure about it, this is your moment. Read the following and respond with your heart:

> We've all sinned and fall short of God's standard. Your sin has separated you from God, just as it separated me from God. He created us to be in relationship with Him, though. Our lives are broken and empty without Him.
>
> But you can change that. It's up to you. He is waiting for you with open arms. His Son is waiting for you with open arms—the same arms that were spread wide on the cross for you.
>
> God has already completed His part to bring you back: He sent His Son to die on the cross for you. That's not a fairy tale or fantasy. It happened. It's a historical fact. Jesus bled and died on the cross so you can live. Your sins were nailed with Him to that cross two thousand years ago.
>
> It is finished. He has accomplished everything for you. Your sins have already been atoned for. They've been forgiven. They've even been forgotten. They've been cast as far as the east is from the west.
>
> How are you feeling?

Do you believe that Jesus died for you on that cross. That His blood washed away your sins—that His blood has washed *you* white as snow? That He was buried in a tomb? And then rose again to new life three days later?

If you believe this, if you truly believe what Jesus did for you on the cross, then you are saved!

And the angels in heaven REJOICE with you!!! And so do I. You are not alone in this moment. You have also been baptized into the Body of Christ! You are at one with every other saved Christian in the world! Welcome to the family!

Let me say that again: WELCOME TO THE FAMILY!

You are fully and completely forgiven of all your sins, every one of them—past, present, and future! There is *nothing* else for you to do to be saved. And there is absolutely *nothing* you can do to be *more* saved.

You are also sealed for eternity. Your sins are forgiven and forgotten. You are once again in right standing with God. Your sins have been washed whiter than snow. You have resurrected to new life just like Jesus was. The old you has died and the new you has risen with Christ.

You also have the Holy Spirit living in you. You can trust God that He is there dwelling in you. Listen for Him. Listen to Him. Talk with Him. Ask Him questions. He will guide you and lead you further and further away from sin and closer and closer to God, Jesus, and His righteousness.

Take a few minutes to talk with God now. Let Him know how you feel in this moment. Praise Him. Thank Him. Worship Him in whatever way you feel led.

If you would like to say a prayer and don't have the words you want to express, here is a brief one for you. Remember that this isn't a prayer for salvation. You are already saved. This is a prayer of thanksgiving and rejoicing in what God and Jesus have already done for you!

> Heavenly Father, thank You for not giving up on me. Thank You for leading me back to You. It's where I need to be. It's where I want to be. With You. With Your Son in my heart. Your Holy Spirit in me and guiding me.
>
> Thank You for sending Your Son to die for me so I can have new life. I see it now. I see what You did for me. I see what Your Son did for me. I believe it. I believe it with my whole heart. I surrender my life to You, to Your Son. I choose to live for You from this moment forward. Thank You, Abba Father.
>
> In Jesus's precious name I pray, amen.

Finally, if you haven't already, find a local church to attend. Preferably an independent, nondenominational church. One that believes in the power of the Holy Spirit through Spirit baptism. And get involved in a Bible study with other believers who will help you (and you can help them) read and understand God's Word. Find a group that studies all of scripture, but especially one that studies Paul's letters since he is our apostle for today.

Now… are you ready to get wet?

9

How to Be Baptized in Water

JESUS SPENT THREE days in the grave. When you get water-baptized, you won't even be in the water for three seconds! But even though you're immersed for just a few seconds, it's a great way to celebrate your faith in His death, burial, and resurrection.

But before you get wet, it's important to understand the biblical reasons for water baptism and reasons some people use that aren't biblical.

Water baptism doesn't save you or make you more saved. It doesn't wash away your sins. It doesn't make you a new person. All of that happened in the moment of your salvation, when you believed in your heart that Jesus died for you, shed His blood for you, to atone for your sins. You are already saved and in Christ!

> Therefore if anyone is in Christ, this person is a new creation; the old things passed away; behold, new things have come. (2 Corinthians 5:17)

Water baptism also doesn't get you into heaven; the blood of Jesus and grace of God have already done that for you. It is also not a necessary step to join a church. This is not biblical in any way.

So, at your water baptism, you are simply professing in public that, because of what Christ did for you on the cross, you are forgiven, forever saved, and forever free.

There is no other requirement for being baptized in water. You only need to be saved, which is believing in the gospel as found in 1 Corinthians 15:1-4.

You can be baptized by any other believer in Jesus Christ. It does not need to be a pastor or ordained minister. It can be a relative or friend in Christ.

You also don't need to be baptized in a church building or during a church service (though most people are). Water baptism can be in any body of water where you are able to be fully immersed. So, it can be in a church baptismal, big tub of water, swimming pool, pond, lake, river, or ocean. It just doesn't matter. The important part is your public profession of your new faith in Jesus Christ and the beautiful memory of replicating your Savior's death, burial, and resurrection.

Water baptisms today are not for any spiritual purpose, although they can certainly feel spiritual—and perhaps should. During a water baptism, you as a believer are not filled with any spiritual power and do not receive any spiritual gifts. That only happens at salvation and Spirit baptisms. Water baptisms are simply a physical representation of a heart decision to believe in Jesus as the One who died to atone for your sins so that you can one day stand before God sin free.

And you only need to be baptized in water just one time. There is no biblical reason to experience more than one water baptism.

While water baptism isn't part of the salvation process, making a public profession of faith is a weighty decision not to be taken lightly. It's also not the end of the process. Rather, it's the continuation of your new life in Christ, one that began with your decision to believe in Him.

If you are being water-baptized at a church, they may ask you to meet with a pastor first. They will want to know that you understand the purpose of water baptism and that you understand and have experienced biblical salvation. This is a good practice that will provide great encouragement for your decision. It will also help build the church on a solid foundation of true faith and likewise build up the greater Body of Christ as well.

Just before you are baptized, you may be asked to give a personal testimony. Public speaking is easy for some but difficult for others. If the idea of giving a public testimony makes you want to slide into the water and stay there, I suggest coming up with a simple sentence or two that is easy to memorize. Even saying a few words will make your baptism experience even more memorable.

Here are some words you can begin with, but be sure to make them your own:

> I love Jesus and know that He died on the cross to take my sins away. He was buried in the grave. And three days later He rose again. The Holy Spirit is in my heart and will help me live my life for Jesus.

In the Water

After you have stepped into the water, the person baptizing you should ask you some questions and then baptize you with specific words.

The questions will be something like:

- Do you believe with your whole heart that Jesus died on the cross for your sins?
- Do you believe that He was buried and rose again three days later?
- Are you a new creation in Christ?
- Do you understand that, along with your faith, you were saved by the grace of God alone and nothing else?
- Are you ready to live for Jesus the rest of your life?

Before the baptizer immerses you in the water, they will say something like: "On the basis of your personal decision to believe in Jesus Christ, it is my honor to baptize you in the name of the Father, the Son, and the Holy Spirit."

And then everyone cheers!

Beyond the Cross

Please don't stop at the cross—at your salvation and water baptism. Keep going! All believers need to move beyond the cross that saved them.

Get to know the Holy Spirit. God sent Him to be your guide when Jesus ascended to heaven. Don't ignore Him or quench Him. Let Him guide and help you every day in your faith journey.

Pray always, both in your own words and in the Spirit. Read and study the Bible so you can grow in faith. While all of scripture is helpful for learning and growing in faith, the most important books for followers of Jesus today in this age of grace are Paul's letters—Romans through Philemon.

And, of course, receive the baptism in the Holy Spirit.

Now... are you ready to catch that fire?

10

How to Be Baptized in the Holy Spirit

THE DISCIPLES HAD the Holy Spirit with them, then in them, then upon them. Jesus spoke these words to them just prior to His arrest in the Garden of Gethsemane:

> I will ask the Father, and He will give you another Helper, so that He may be with you forever; the Helper is the Spirit of truth, whom the world cannot receive, because it does not see Him or know Him; but you know Him because He remains with you and will be in you. (John 14:16-17)

Then, three days later, in John 20:22 (on the day of His resurrection), Jesus breathed on the disciples and told them to "receive the Holy Spirit." That is the moment the Holy Spirit went into and indwelled the disciples.

Forty days after Jesus rose from the dead, and immediately before His ascension to heaven, He spoke again to the disciples:

> Gathering them together, He commanded them not to leave Jerusalem, but to wait for what the Father had promised, "Which," He said, "you heard of from Me; for John baptized with water, but you will be baptized with the Holy Spirit not many days from now.... but you will receive power when the Holy Spirit has come upon you; and you shall be My witnesses both in Jerusalem and in all Judea, and Samaria, and as far as the remotest part of the earth." (Acts 1:4-5, 8)

As Jesus promised, the Holy Spirit was already *with them*, would be *in them* (when Jesus breathed on them), and would then come *upon them* (ten days later at Pentecost)!

This is so amazing and yet so powerful. Jesus—God's incarnated Word—is clear: Receiving the indwelling of the Holy Spirit at salvation and being baptized in the Holy Spirit are two separate and distinct experiences.

Nowhere in scripture did God end Spirit baptism. Nowhere. We are to read Paul's writings and follow him, *just as he followed Jesus*:

> And you should imitate me, just as I imitate Christ. (1 Corinthians 11:1 NLT)

Once again, Paul received his writings directly by revelation from Jesus Himself:

> Dear brothers and sisters, I want you to understand that the gospel message I preach is not based on mere human reasoning. I received my message from

no human source, and no one taught me. Instead, I received it by direct revelation from Jesus Christ. (Galatians 1:11-12 NLT)

So, follow Paul and his writings just as he followed Jesus. And this includes the baptism in the Holy Spirit.

As I've reiterated throughout this book, Paul is our apostle for today. He believed in baptism in the Holy Spirit. Jesus also believed in and experienced this baptism—His Father performed it on Him after His water baptism in the Jordan River.

Paul also baptized others in the Holy Spirit. While this book doesn't delve into the baptisms that Paul experienced himself, Acts 9 records that he was filled with the Holy Spirit (baptized in the Holy Spirit) and baptized in water by Ananias. Scripture does not clearly tell us when or where he was "saved." I personally believe that both his salvation baptism and Spirit baptism occurred when Jesus struck Him blind on the road to Damascus:

> So Ananias departed and entered the house, and after laying his hands on him said, "Brother Saul, the Lord Jesus, who appeared to you on the road by which you were coming, has sent me so that you may regain your sight and be filled with the Holy Spirit." And immediately something like fish scales fell from his eyes, and he regained his sight, and he got up and was baptized. (Acts 9:17-18)

Understand also that Paul would not have been able to baptize others in the Holy Spirit if he had not experienced it himself.

Here's a good analogy: Imagine you are at home sitting at a table or standing at your kitchen counter. It's just you and a refreshing glass of water in front of you. At this point, the water is *with* you. If you drink it, the water is now *in* you. Afterward, the water is both with you and in you. But Jesus also promised that Holy Spirit would come *upon* you as well, that you would be immersed in Him and His power.

The only way to be immersed in the figurative water (Holy Spirit) is to leave your comfort zone—the comfort of your "home." Unfortunately, this is where most believers stay: in the comfort of their safe Christian life—the Holy Spirit with them and in them, but not upon them with power.

So, freely receive the baptism in the Holy Spirit. It will be your chance to spiritually go jump in a divine "lake" and immerse yourself in Him. To soak in Him as He soaks into you. Let Him saturate your body, soul, and spirit. Surrender your spirit fully to Him. Your will. And your life.

Let yourself be fully immersed with the power of the Holy Spirit, who is the mighty Spirit of God.

You won't lose control of yourself, I promise. That is not how He operates. The Holy Spirit will work His gifts in you and through you *in His time* and *at His will*—when He chooses. Your role is to surrender to Him and not prevent Him from working.

Receive the Baptism in the Holy Spirit

You can receive your Spirit baptism from Jesus by yourself, or from a pastor or other believer who's received their Spirit baptism. They just need to fully believe in this baptism. Just as you received Christ by faith, you also receive the power of the

Holy Spirit by faith. And that means anyone with you needs to have that same strength of faith.

As I mentioned in the Introduction, I received my Spirit baptism all by myself watching a seven-year-old sermon on TV. I had never heard of this baptism, but as soon as that preacher asked if anyone wanted to receive the baptism in the Holy Spirit, I said, "Yes!" Then I stood up in my living room and followed his directions. I believed and received in that moment.

No one was with me. No one laid hands on me. I simply asked Jesus to baptize me in the Holy Spirit and trusted that He would, and He fulfilled His promise.

I had absolutely no idea what to expect. I did not understand the private prayer language or the Holy Spirit's supernatural gifts. But just as with the immature, messed-up believers at Corinth, He still worked His supernatural gifts in me and through me even though I didn't understand them. And that's a good thing, because it means I can't brag that they are my gifts or abilities that I can call up and use anytime I want, like Superman dispatching his super-strength or x-ray vision whenever he wants. I can't. And thank God for that!

Are you ready to receive your free gift from Jesus?

Here we go!

Stand up.

Hold your hands out and facing up, like you're about to receive a gift, because you are.

Say the following words out loud. This is not a prayer but a request you have of your Savior:

> Lord Jesus, thank You for choosing to die on the cross for me. Because You surrendered Your life for me, I am saved and sealed for eternity. Thank You for saving me and thank You for Your Holy Spirit in me.
>
> Jesus, I surrender my life to You. I let go of my life and put it in Your hands. I empty myself for You. I ask You now to baptize me in your Holy Spirit. Immerse my body, my soul, and my spirit with Your Spirit. Let Your Spirit come upon me and wash over me. Fill me completely from the top of my head to the soles of my feet. Immerse me in the power of Your Spirit. Anoint me right now with His power, with His holy fire. Thank You, Lord Jesus. Thank You.

If you feel words or sounds coming up from inside you, just let them out. Don't worry at all what it might sound like. Just speak the words or the sounds. This is where you need to just trust Jesus and trust the Holy Spirit inside you. Don't quench Him!

If nothing is happening, don't worry, it will. The Holy Spirit works differently in each of us and with different timing.

Now, just thank God. Thank Jesus. Praise Them. Worship Them. There are no right words; there is no perfect response. Just speak from your new heart.

Full of Yourself—or Full of the Holy Spirit?

Unlike your salvation and water baptisms, there is no limit to how many times you can be baptized with the Holy Spirit. And that is a good thing. We only need to be saved once.

Sealed once. Placed into the Body of Christ once. And water baptism is not a spiritual act, so that, too, is a one-time event.

But we are human. We are flesh. Our mind, emotions, will, and heart are filled with selfishness and worldliness. Jesus wants us to shed all of that. He wants us to empty ourselves.

Being filled with the Holy Spirit requires surrender. Fully surrendering ourselves to God, Jesus, and the Holy Spirit. Unfortunately, surrender takes time. Like, a lifetime. We will never reach full surrender. We're all layered inside and out with too much flesh, too much selfishness, too much world.

You have the Holy Spirit from salvation, but does the Holy Spirit have you? Have you let Him grab you and take control of your life? That is what baptism in the Holy Spirit is about. Surrendering yourself so He can have more of you. More of your heart, soul, spirit, and body.

As you go through times of deeper surrender—and you will—empty more of yourself. Each time you do, you free up more room for the Holy Spirit to fill you. So, don't hesitate to ask Jesus for another baptism with the Holy Spirit. He won't deny you:

> So if you, despite being evil, know how to give good gifts to your children, how much more will your heavenly Father give the Holy Spirit to those who ask Him? (Luke 11:13)

What exactly are you surrendering? Anything and everything in your life that you place above your Savior. Anything that you are holding on to that prevents you from growing in Christ. It might seem like a short list at first, but I promise you, over time, you'll realize just how much we all put above our Jesus, and how far we push Him down our priority list.

Your list will include your lifestyle, what you put into your body, what you let into your mind, where you spend your time, what you spend your money on, your family, your relationships, your career, past decisions, past hurts, regrets, unforgiveness, bitterness, envy, strife, and on and on.

John the Baptist said it best:

> He must increase, but I must decrease. (John 3:30)

As you grow in Christ and in faith and trust, you will see the need for less and less of yourself. Less and less of your fleshly desires and what the world offers. Notice these moments. Never hesitate to ask Jesus to baptize you again with the Holy Spirit. Do this whenever you're ready for less of you and more of Him.

A Final Word: From My Heart to Yours

I learned so late in life that I can't save myself. That all my striving not to sin still brought sin. That my sea of struggles was never God punishing me, but Him trying to reach me and teach me.

He cared about me and wanted the best for me. He had already forgiven all my sins, but I thought that He only saw one thing when he looked at me—my sins. I was wrong. Instead, He only saw Jesus—His perfect, sinless Son. I see that now. If you are in Christ, that is also how He sees you—a perfect, sinless child of God.

I also see that freedom is in Christ alone. Not in anyone else. Certainly not in myself. I tried creating my own freedom but continually failed. Look away from yourself. Seek Him and you will find freedom you never imagined.

Finally, I also now understand that the Bible isn't about me. It never was. I was never going to find myself in it. We will only find Jesus in it because it is only about Him. Every page, every story points to Him, our Savior. It's simply a love letter. He wrote it to me, and He wrote it to you. I live in total awe and wonder at the tortuous sacrifice He made to make sure I know how much He loves me and that I read His letter.

In His Love,
John

www.ingramcontent.com/pod-product-compliance
Lightning Source LLC
Chambersburg PA
CBHW072149070526
44585CB00015B/1064